CIMA

Strategic Level

P3

Risk Management

Exam Practice Kit

For exams from January 2021

Sixth edition 2020

ISBN 9781 5097 3636 2
e-ISBN 9781 5097 3672 0

British Library Cataloguing-in-Publication Data
A catalogue record for this book
is available from the British Library

Published by

BPP Learning Media Ltd
BPP House, Aldine Place, 142/144 Uxbridge Road
London W12 8AA

www.bpp.com/learningmedia

Printed in the United Kingdom

Your learning materials, published by BPP Learning Media Ltd, are printed on paper obtained from traceable, sustainable sources.

We are grateful to the Chartered Institute of Management Accountants for allowing us to reproduce extracts from the CIMA exam blueprint. An up-to-date version of the full blueprint is available at www.cimaglobal.com/examblueprints.

Contents

Question and answer index

BPP LEARNING MEDIA

Using your BPP Exam Practice Kit

One of the key criteria for achieving exam success is question practice. There is generally a direct correlation between candidates who study all topics and practise exam questions and those who are successful in their real exams. This Kit gives you ample opportunity for such practice throughout your preparations for your OT exam.

All questions in your exam are compulsory and all the component learning outcomes will be examined so you must **study the whole syllabus**. Selective studying will limit the number of questions you can answer and hence reduce your chances of passing. It is better to go into the exam knowing a reasonable amount about most of the syllabus rather than concentrating on a few topics to the exclusion of the rest.

Practising as many exam-style questions as possible will be the key to passing this exam. You must do questions under **timed conditions**.

Breadth of question coverage

Questions will cover the whole of the syllabus so you must study all the topics in the syllabus.

The weightings in the table below indicate the approximate proportion of study time you should spend on each topic, and is related to the number of questions per syllabus area in the exam.

P3 Risk Management Syllabus topics	Weighting
A Enterprise risk	25%
B Strategic risk	25%
C Internal controls	25%
D Cyber risk	25%

(CIMA exam blueprint, 2019)

Examination structure

The Objective Test exam

Pass mark	70%
Format	Computer-based assessment
Duration	90 minutes
Number of questions	60
Marking	No partial marking – each question marked correct or incorrect All questions carry the same weighting (ie same marks)
Weighting	As per syllabus areas All representative task statements from the examination blueprint will be covered
Question Types	Multiple choice Multiple response Drag and drop Gap fill Hot spot
Booking availability	On demand
Results	Immediate

What the examiner means

The table below has been prepared by CIMA to further help you interpret the syllabus and learning outcomes and the meaning of questions.

You will see that there are five skills levels you may be expected to demonstrate, ranging from Remembering and Understanding to Evaluation. CIMA Certificate subjects only use levels 1 to 3, but in CIMA's Professional qualification the entire hierarchy will be used.

Skills level		Verbs used	Definition
Level 5	**Evaluation** *The examination or assessment of problems, and use of judgment to draw conclusions*	Advise	Counsel, inform or notify
		Assess	Evaluate or estimate the nature, ability or quality of
		Evaluate	Appraise or assess the value of
		Recommend	Propose a course of action
		Review	Assess and evaluate in order, to change if necessary
		Select	Choose an option or course of action after consideration of the alternatives

	Skills level	Verbs used	Definition
Level 4	**Analysis** *The examination and study of the interrelationships of separate areas in order to identify causes and find evidence to support inferences*	Align	Arrange in an orderly way
		Analyse	Examine in detail the structure of
		Communicate	Share or exchange information
		Compare and contrast	Show the similarities and/or differences between
		Develop	Grow and expand a concept
		Discuss	Examine in detail by argument
		Examine	Inspect thoroughly
		Monitor	Observe and check the progress of
		Prioritise	Place in order of priority or sequence for action
		Produce	Create or bring into existence
Level 3	**Application** *The use or demonstration of knowledge, concepts or techniques*	Apply	Put to practical use
		Calculate	Ascertain or reckon mathematically
		Conduct	Organise and carry out
		Demonstrate	Prove with certainty or exhibit by practical means
		Determine	Ascertain or establish exactly by research or calculation
		Perform	Carry out, accomplish, or fulfil
		Prepare	Make or get ready for use
		Reconcile	Make or prove consistent/compatible
		Record	Keep a permanent account of facts, events or transactions
		Use	Apply a technique or concept
Level 1/2	**Remembering and understanding** *The perception and comprehension of the significance of an area utilising knowledge gained*	Define	Give the exact meaning of
		Describe	Communicate the key features of
		Distinguish	Highlight the differences between
		Explain	Make clear or intelligible/state the meaning or purpose of
		Identify	Recognise, establish or select after consideration
		Illustrate	Use an example to describe or explain something

Skills level		Verbs used	Definition
		List	Make a list of
		Recognise	Identify/recall
		State	Express, fully or clearly, the details/facts of
		Outline	Give a summary of
		Understand	Comprehend ideas, concepts and techniques

(CIMA exam blueprint, 2019)

How to pass

Good exam technique

The best approach to the computer-based assessment (CBA)

You're not likely to have a great deal of spare time during the CBA itself, so you must make sure you don't waste a single minute.

You should:

1 Click 'Next' for any that have long scenarios or are very complex and return to these later

2 When you reach the 60th question, use the Review Screen to return to any questions you skipped past or any you flagged for review

Here's how the tools in the exam will help you to do this in a controlled and efficient way.

The 'Next' button

What does it do? This will move you on to the next question whether or not you have completed the one you are on.

When should I use it? Use this to move through the exam on your first pass through if you encounter a question that you suspect is going to take you a long time to answer. The Review Screen (see below) will help you to return to these questions later in the exam.

The 'Flag for Review' button

What does it do? This button will turn the icon yellow and when you reach the end of the exam questions you will be told that you have flagged specific questions for review. If the exam time runs out before you have reviewed any flagged questions, they will be submitted as they are.

When should I use it? Use this when you've answered a question but you're not completely comfortable with your answer. If there is time left at the end, you can quickly come back via the Review Screen (see below), but if time runs out at least it will submit your current answer. Do not use the Flag for Review button too often or you will end up with too long a list to review at the end. Important note –studies have shown that you are usually best to stick with your first instincts!

The Review Screen

What does it do? This screen appears after you click 'Next' on the 60th question. It shows you any incomplete questions and any you have flagged for review. It allows you to jump back to specific questions **or** work through all your incomplete questions **or** work through all your flagged for review questions.

When should I use it? As soon as you've completed your first run through the exam and reached the 60th question. The very first thing to do is to work through all your incomplete questions as they will all be marked as incorrect if you don't submit an answer for these in the remaining time. Importantly, this will also help to pick up any questions you thought you'd completed but didn't answer properly (eg you only picked two answer options in a multi-response question that required three answers to be selected). After you've submitted answers for all your incomplete questions you should use the Review Screen to work through all the questions you flagged for review.

The different Objective Test question types

Passing your CBA is all about demonstrating your understanding of the technical syllabus content. You will find this easier to do if you are comfortable with the different types of Objective Test questions that you will encounter in the CBA, especially if you have a practised approach to each one.

You will find yourself continuously practising these styles of questions throughout your Objective Test programme. This way you will check and reinforce your technical knowledge at the same time as becoming more and more comfortable with your approach to each style of question.

Multiple choice

Standard multiple choice items provide four options. One option is correct and the other three are incorrect. Incorrect options will be plausible, so you should expect to have to use detailed, syllabus-specific knowledge to identify the correct answer rather than relying on common sense.

Multiple response

A multiple response item is the same as a multiple choice question, except **more than one** response is required. You will normally (but not always) be told how many options you need to select.

Drag and drop

Drag and drop questions require you to drag a 'token' onto a pre-defined area. These tokens can be images or text. This type of question is effective at testing the order of events, labelling a diagram or linking events to outcomes.

Gap fill

Gap fill (or 'fill in the blank') questions require you to type a short numerical response. You should carefully follow the instructions in the question in terms of how to type your answer – eg the correct number of decimal places.

Hot spot

These questions require you to identify an area or location on an image by clicking on it. This is commonly used to identify a specific point on a graph or diagram.

A final word on time management

Time does funny things in an exam!

Scientific studies have shown that humans have great difficulty in judging how much time has passed if they are concentrating fully on a challenging task (which your CBA should be!).

You can try this for yourself. Have a go at, say, five questions for your paper, and notice what time you start at. As soon as you finish the last question try to estimate how long it took you and then compare to your watch. The majority of us tend to underestimate how quickly time passes and this can cost you dearly in a full exam if you don't take steps to keep track of time.

So, the key thing here is to set yourself sensible milestones, and then get into the habit of regularly checking how you are doing against them:

- You need to develop an internal warning system – 'I've now spent more than three minutes on this one calculation – this is too long and I need to move on!' (less for a narrative question!)
- Keep your milestones in mind (eg approximately 30 questions done after 45 mins). If you are a distance from where you should be then adjust your pace accordingly. This usually means speeding up but can mean slowing down a bit if needs be, as you may be rushing when you don't need to and increasing the risk of making silly mistakes.

A full exam will be a mix of questions you find harder and those you find easier, and in the real CBA the order is randomised, so you could get a string of difficult questions right at the beginning of your exam. Do not be put off by this – they should be balanced later by a series of questions you find easier.

Objective test questions

1 Risk and Risk Exposure

1.1 Company P is a market leading manufacturer of flatscreen televisions and is considering the introduction of full automation into its factories. Currently, components including circuit boards, wiring, cases and screens are sourced from separate suppliers and then individually assembled by hand in their factory. However, concerns over build quality have emerged in recent consumer testing and automation is being considered as a solution to this problem.

Which ONE of the following options describes the most likely interaction between risks at Company P from the decision to automate production?

- ○ Machine failure risk increases and human error risk falls
- ○ Labour costs rise and are replaced by higher costs of depreciation
- ○ Labour costs fall and manufacturing speed increases
- ○ Build quality increases and sales improve

1.2 **Which of the following statements about risk are true?**

1 A speculative risk is a risk from which either good or harm may result.

2 A fundamental risk is a risk beyond the control of any individual.

- ○ Statement 1 true; Statement 2 true.
- ○ Statement 1 true; Statement 2 false.
- ○ Statement 1 false; Statement 2 true.
- ○ Statement 1 false; Statement 2 false.

1.3 **Which ONE of the following statements is true?**

- ○ Risk is only concerned about things going wrong.
- ○ Risk only relates to new issues.
- ○ Big enterprises are the only ones who need to manage risks.
- ○ Risk can recognise positive events, including opportunities.

1.4 **Choose a word from the list below to complete the statement.**

Risk analysis is about ranking the impact and [▼] of a risk occurring.

Pull down list:

result
likelihood
cost
opportunity

1.5 **Which ONE of the following risks is most likely to be classified as a strategic risk?**

- ○ A merger between the business's sole supplier of one component and the business's main competitor.
- ○ The insolvency of one of the business's 15 suppliers of a particular component.
- ○ One of the business's most significant customers seeking to extend its credit period from 30 to 40 days.
- ○ One of the business's most significant suppliers transferring its manufacturing operations overseas to a developed country.

1.6 'A modelling and risk assessment procedure in which changes are made to significant variables in order to determine the effect of these changes on the planned outcome.'

What is this describing?

- ○ Value at risk
- ○ Sensitivity analysis
- ○ Expected value
- ○ Certainty equivalent

1.7 **Which ONE of the following is NOT a technique for measuring risk?**

- ○ Risk mapping
- ○ Sensitivity analysis
- ○ Standard deviation of expected returns
- ○ Variance

1.8 Company A is a geological exploration company. It is considering a speculative investment which will require drilling in a location where it is believed a rare mineral exists. However, estimates of volume and quality have not been fully confirmed and there is only a 60% chance that the ore extracted each year will be valuable enough to sell for $800,000. Otherwise, the company will only be able to sell the lower grade output for $300,000 each year. The proposed extraction site has great cultural significance to the local population and so the company has negotiated a fixed term for the project of only five years and has committed to make good any damage to the site. Although estimates of costs have been hard to quantify, Company A has initially forecast an amount of $200,000 for site restoration at the end of the project and believes that the cost of this investment will be $2 million.

Assuming a cost of capital of 12% and working in $'000 to one decimal place, what will be the sensitivity to the project of a 20% increase in the costs required to repair the drill site at the end of the investment?

- ○ 45.8%
- ○ 124.0%
- ○ 1,217.6%
- ○ 218.5%

1.9 Company S delivers parcels for a large online retail company, Company O, which accounts for 95% of its revenue. Company S's operations are very efficient and it consistently rates highly with Company O's customers for the courtesy of its drivers and the timeliness of its deliveries from its owned fleet of modern vehicles.

Your colleague has been tasked with looking at risk management for Company S but is struggling to see where the company has any weaknesses that might expose it to risk.

Based on the information given, which ONE of the following should your colleague consider?

○ Operational issues

○ Supplier power

○ Buyer power

○ Increases in interest rates

1.10 J is the manager at Company L. He has been asked to look at risk management in his department, which processes supplier invoices for payment. He has identified the following risks that could occur:

- Mistakes being made by the newly recruited purchase ledger clerk
- Fictitious suppliers being set up on the system for payment
- Supplier invoices and statements being lost
- Supplier bank details not being kept up to date
- Backups not being made regularly
- Inadequate segregation of duties

Which ONE of the following should J do next?

○ Redesign the company's internal control systems

○ Assess the significance of each risk

○ Work out how each risk should be managed

○ Implement new internal controls in his department

○ Pass his findings on to the board of directors

1.11 Company H makes agricultural machinery. It makes a range of machines and other agricultural equipment in its home country, and all of its products are sold in its home market. It has a strong place in this market, but it has several competitors who sell similar machinery.

Which of the following would normally be classified as a strategic risk for the company?

Select ALL that apply.

☐ The risk that a new type of irrigation system will fail to find a large enough market

☐ The risk of competitors moving their production to a different country and being able to cut costs

☐ The risk that the human resources director will be recruited by Company T, a key competitor

☐ The risk of resource depletion, meaning that new sources of sheet metal will have to be found

---

1.12 In recent years, ABC Bank has responded to a rise in commercial property prices and the demand from real estate companies for commercial property loans. It now has a large portfolio of property loans, and a strong capital base. Many loans are at a fixed rate of interest and in a foreign currency (US dollars). The board of directors is alarmed by a report suggesting that property prices have risen too far, and a collapse in prices could be imminent.

What are the main risk exposures faced by the bank with regard to its commercial property lending?

Select ALL that apply.

- ☐ Credit risk
- ☐ Reputation risk
- ☐ Interest rate risk
- ☐ Currency risk

1.13 BM is a food manufacturer in a developed country that supplies a wide variety of customers in its domestic market and a small number of selected customers overseas. The board of directors at BM has decided to appoint a risk manager whose first job is to list all the major risks that the company faces. Having looked at the job description for the position, the risk manager has been asked to clarify the difference between strategic and operational risks.

Which of the following is an example of a strategic risk for BM?

Select ALL that apply.

- ☐ Increasing sensitivity of consumers to food allergies
- ☐ Consumer resistance to testing their products using animals
- ☐ Failure to label foods accurately for nutritional information
- ☐ Power cuts interrupting production at the factory
- ☐ Resignation of any factory workers on moral or ethical grounds

---

1.14 **Which ONE of these risks would be classified as a risk faced ONLY by an international business?**

- ○ Market risk
- ○ Political risk
- ○ Credit risk
- ○ Cultural risk

1.15 You work in the finance department of a large retailer as a financial analyst. One of your responsibilities is to prepare high-level commentary for the investor relations department of the company. Within the annual summary information provided by the chief accountant, you note that trade receivables have increased from $20 million to $30 million, while revenue has increased from $100 million to $175 million.

From the following statements, which ONE is the MOST plausible explanation for these amounts?

- ○ A sales initiative offering a prompt payment discount
- ○ New staff in credit control are taking time to settle in to their new role
- ○ Reduction in demand for products
- ○ Credit terms have been increased to stimulate demand

1.16 A recent change of government in Country X has led to an increase in the statutory minimum wage and greater protection for employees via enhanced workplace legislation.

What is the MOST LIKELY implication of these two events for a construction company based in Country X?

- ○ Increased staff turnover rates
- ○ Adverse material usage variances
- ○ Improved profitability on contracts
- ○ Adverse labour cost variances

1.17 **Which ONE of the following risks could be described as a pure risk?**

- ○ A dramatic fall in the value of shares across a stock market
- ○ Losing a patent held by a manufacturer
- ○ Loss of all data from a malicious computer virus
- ○ Restriction of funds from an entity's bank

1.18 E is a publishing company based in a developing country which operates on the 15th floor of a new office. It has decided to draw up a risk map showing its primary risks and is preparing to report them as part of its governance responsibilities. It will use likelihood and impact to assess its risks.

From the pull down list, match each of the following risks with the relevant risk map assessment.

High likelihood, low impact	**High likelihood, high impact**
▼	▼
Low likelihood, low impact	**Low likelihood, high impact**
▼	▼

Pull down list:

Staff are unable to come into work due to sickness
Staff create content that breaks copyright laws and the company is sued for damages
Staff are unable to access the office because the lift malfunctions
Staff cannot access their work because of a fire in the server room

---

1.19 Company C is a manufacturer of fizzy drinks. Over the summer, there is a prolonged period of hot weather in the country where Company C is based. During that same period, the factory which supplies carbon dioxide to drinks manufacturers including Company C closes down for three weeks to upgrade its machinery. Consequently, there is a well-publicised shortfall of carbon dioxide which is used in the manufacture of fizzy drinks.

Which of the following statements correctly describes the likely impact of these two events on Company C?

Select ALL that apply.

☐ Increased demand for its drinks

☐ Increased prices of its drinks

☐ Increased sales of its drinks

☐ Increased production of its drinks

☐ Increased competition in the soft drinks sector

---

2 Managing Risk

2.1 **Which of the following groups should the management of an organisation report its risks to?**

Select ALL that apply.

☐ Shareholders

☐ Lenders

☐ Customers

☐ Suppliers

☐ Government

☐ Employees

2.2 Risk mapping is a technique for assessing the severity of a risk and the probability or frequency of its likely occurrence.

For what type of risk would it probably be most appropriate to take out an insurance policy from an insurance company?

○ Severity low, frequency low

○ Severity high, frequency low

○ Severity high, frequency high

○ Severity low, frequency high

2.3 **Which ONE of the following definitions best describes risk aversion?**

○ Avoiding investments where the risk is high if an investment offering the same return for less risk is available

○ Trying to reduce or minimise risks through risk management

○ Avoiding risks by refusing to invest in high-risk projects or investments

○ Investing in projects offering the highest expected value of net present value

---

2.4 D is a manufacturer that is experiencing some problems with defects in one of its main products. The product, which has been made by the company for many years and is very profitable, has generated over 2,000 customer complaints in the last month (around 10% of products sold) which presents a reputation risk for D.

Which ONE of the following risk mitigation strategies should D follow?

- ○ Accept this risk: the company makes other products which are just as profitable
- ○ Reduce the risk by increasing the frequency of maintenance on the production line manufacturing the affected product
- ○ Transfer the risk by outsourcing the manufacture of the product to another company
- ○ Avoid the risk by ceasing production while the cause of the defects is identified

---

2.5 B produces financial information to monitor its position and performance. Each indicator is plotted on a quarterly basis to show a profile that the Finance Director can use to assess the company's risks. The following data have been extracted from the most recent set of management accounts:

	Quarter 1	*Quarter 2*	*Quarter 3*	*Quarter 4*
Receivables days	30 days	31 days	38 days	41 days
Gearing ratio	51%	57%	62%	69%
Interest cover	4.1	4.0	3.9	2.7

For each of the indicators below, suggest an appropriate risk response for the Finance Director to take from the pull down list. Each response should be different.

Receivables days [▼]

Gearing ratio [▼]

Pull down list:

Transfer
Avoid
Reduce
Accept

2.6 **Which ONE of the following is NOT part of the control environment?**

- ○ The operating style of managers and directors
- ○ Access restrictions on assets
- ○ The directors' methods of imposing control
- ○ The integrity, ethical values and competence of directors and staff

---

2.7 RLJ manufactures high-performance sports cars.

For the following risks, suggest techniques for mitigating each one using the pull down list:

A customer or third party may be killed or injured by an accident caused by a manufacturing flaw.

[▼]

Environmental legislation in Germany is likely to require cars sold there to comply with stringent emissions and fuel economy standards that are impossible for cars of this type.

[▼]

Pull down list:

Transfer
Accept
Avoid
Reduce

2.8 **Which ONE of the following statements is true?**

- ○ Risk hedging is taking action to offset one risk by incurring a new risk in the opposite direction.
- ○ High frequency, high severity risks are always strategic risks.
- ○ Risk transfer means the management of a portfolio of different risks.
- ○ Insuring risks means that businesses will not need to take any measures to reduce those risks.

2.9 Risk appetite is the nature and strength of risk that an organisation is prepared to bear.

Which TWO of the following terms are examples of risk appetite?

- ☐ Risk tolerance
- ☐ Risk seeking
- ☐ Risk aversion
- ☐ Risk capacity

2.10 A reputable food manufacturer produces a popular snack that is sold across the world and targeted at both families and individuals. It carries a warning label on the packet stating that the snack contains nuts which can cause an allergic reaction in some cases and that anyone who is considering eating this snack should be aware of the ingredients so they are aware of the possible side-effects from any allergy they may have.

What kind of risk management strategy is the manufacturer of this snack using?

Select ONE of the following options:

- ○ Transfer
- ○ Avoid
- ○ Reduce
- ○ Accept

2.11 **Which of the following are components of the Committee of Sponsoring Organisations (COSO) Enterprise Risk Management framework?**

Select ALL that apply.

- ☐ Information, communication and reporting
- ☐ Governance and culture
- ☐ Internal audit
- ☐ Strategy and objective setting
- ☐ Monitoring activities
- ☐ Performance
- ☐ Project management
- ☐ Review and revision

2.12 **Which ONE of the following issues related to risk management will the COSO enterprise risk management framework NOT help to address?**

- ○ Helping an organisation decide whether to reduce, eliminate or transfer a particular risk
- ○ Management of the risks associated with stakeholder conflicts
- ○ Allocation of resources to suitable projects
- ○ Embedding risk management in the culture of the organisation

---

2.13 A hospital has a very good record of treating and discharging its patients quickly, but it is very dependent upon its IT systems to make sure that this record is maintained. In recent years there have not been any IT system breakdowns that have adversely affected patient care. The hospital has compiled a risk map and identified the risk of a breakdown in its IT systems as being of high severity, but low frequency.

How should the hospital respond to this risk?

Select ALL that apply.

- ☐ Outsource its IT function
- ☐ Make sure that contingency plans and procedures are in place and well understood
- ☐ Keep the situation under review
- ☐ Close the departments that would be the most severely affected by any IT breakdown

---

2.14 Projects involve risk and risk management.

The taking out of an insurance policy is an example of risk:

- ○ Reduction
- ○ Transfer
- ○ Acceptance
- ○ Avoidance

2.15 **Which of the following would be considered the behaviour of a 'good corporate citizen'?**

Select ALL that apply.

- ☐ Paying unskilled employees a 'living wage' in excess of the minimum wage
- ☐ Sponsoring a local children's sports team
- ☐ Encouraging a 'work-hard play-hard' culture for employees
- ☐ Relocating a customer service call centre to an area with high unemployment
- ☐ Reducing the risk of a component failing by importing the component

---

2.16 A CIMA member suspects fraudulent activity involving a significant sum, but does not have sufficient evidence to be 100% sure a fraud has been committed.

What should the member do?

- ○ Identify the key facts and ethical issues and consider alternative courses of action.
- ○ Spend time observing the suspect and the areas of the business involved to gather further evidence.
- ○ Take no action.
- ○ Confront the suspect immediately and request an explanation.

2.17 ISO 31000 *Risk Management* is a standardised approach to risk management. It contains a series of principles, a framework for implementing these principles and an iterative process for managing risk.

From the following list, identify which ones are included in the risk management principles within ISO 31000 *Risk Management*.

Select ALL that apply.

- ☐ Proportionate to the level of risk faced
- ☐ Communication and consultation
- ☐ Comprehensive
- ☐ Dynamic and responsive to emerging risks
- ☐ Allocation of roles and responsibilities
- ☐ Influence of human and cultural factors

2.18 Risk managers are usually appointed by the board of directors to take the lead on developing best practice on managing risks across the organisation.

From the following list of responsibilities, which are most likely to be undertaken by the risk manager?

Select ALL that apply.

- ☐ Promoting enterprise risk management across the company
- ☐ Developing risk management policies
- ☐ Reviewing existing systems of internal control for risks
- ☐ Designing risk indicators
- ☐ Determining the company's risk appetite

2.19 Organisations use assurance mapping and the three lines of defence model as a structured way of identifying the main sources and types of assurance that they have in place.

Which ONE of the following statements best describes the three lines of defence when used as part of risk management in an organisation?

- ○ Senior management operates the first line of defence, the board operates the second and the third is usually carried out by the external auditors.
- ○ Senior management own and operate the first two lines, while the third line reports directly to the board.
- ○ There is no separation between the first two lines of defence, but the third is managed by a separate part of the organisation.
- ○ The three lines of defence model is used by external auditors to describe the required levels of control when providing assurance on the organisation's financial statements.

2.20 Company C operates a fleet of plant and machinery that is leased to contractors working in the construction industry. The company keeps a risk register which contains the following information:

- Risks by vehicle category
- An indication of the likelihood and impact of each risk
- Staff responsible for managing specific risks
- Quantifications of the costs associated with each risk

Which ONE of the following items would you be most likely to see alongside this information in Company C's risk register?

- ○ Timescales associated with each risk
- ○ Responses to address each risk
- ○ A board sponsor for each risk
- ○ Insurance arrangements for each risk

---

3 Strategy, Reputation and Risk

3.1 F manufactures garden ornaments. The company has recently had to pay compensation to several employees who suffered health problems as result of inhaling cement dust given off by inferior materials during one of the manufacturing processes for its range of garden statues. The company has since improved its internal controls to ensure that this cannot happen again by changing its cement supplier, improving its production processes and amending its health and safety policies to make it clear that all employees engaged in manufacturing must wear protective clothing. These actions have been well publicised in the local community, where F is a major employer.

What types of risk has F reduced by taking this remedial action?

Select ALL that apply.

- ☐ Financial
- ☐ Operational
- ☐ Legal
- ☐ Reputation

3.2 CVJ Ltd manufactures home-cinema equipment which it sells via a network of distributors and other retail outlets. The company has always enjoyed high margins in an industry driven by high-end technology (DVD players and surround sound systems) but more recent developments from digital competitors have revolutionised its market place.

What should CVJ do immediately?

- ○ Outsource all its production to a high-volume low-margin manufacturing facility
- ○ Sell cheaper products under its own brand label
- ○ Complete a review of the marketplace
- ○ Invest in niche segments of the market (eg vinyl records only)

3.3 **The primary purpose of an integrated report is to explain:**

- ○ The organisation's corporate strategy
- ○ How the organisation creates value over time
- ○ How the organisation integrates sustainability and ethics in its strategy
- ○ The organisation's five-year plan

3.4 **Select any concepts that underpin integrated reporting from the list below.**

Select ALL that apply.

- ☐ The value creation process
- ☐ Corporate social responsibility
- ☐ Value creation over time
- ☐ Risk management
- ☐ The capitals

3.5 N is a university located in one medium-sized city in a developed country.

Which of the following assumptions are most relevant to N and its strategy?

Select ALL that apply.

- ☐ A change in national government
- ☐ Changes in local infrastructure, such as roads and telecommunications
- ☐ An increase in digital technology
- ☐ A decline in the birth rate
- ☐ A change in local government

3.6 Company C is a publisher of national newspapers in one developed country and is looking to pursue a corporate objective that will see it become the market leader within three years. In order to achieve this objective, it is looking to formulate a strategy that supports this growth and summarise it in a suitable mission statement. There are currently seven other national newspapers in circulation in the country where C operates, although print media is recognised as being a market in decline.

Which of the following mission statements is most likely to support the strategy that C wishes to pursue?

- ○ We aim to bring you the best newspaper in the country
- ○ We aim to provide you with a low-cost quality newspaper experience
- ○ We want to put the news back in the paper
- ○ We want to put the news in your hand wherever you are

3.7 Company G operates in the technology industry selling apps and computer games. It is currently considered to be a cost leader and wishes to continue this position in the market by maintaining the same strategy over the long term.

Which ONE of the following activities is likely to create the most risk for company G?

- ○ Reducing spending on research and development
- ○ Outsourcing its payroll function to save costs
- ○ Implementing home-working for app developers
- ○ Relocating to smaller premises

3.8 Company M manufactures and sells domestic appliances and wishes to differentiate its products due to their overall superior performance and after-sales customer support. Apart from the obvious capital requirements for manufacture, the market has few barriers to entry and consists of developed and emerging economies across Asia.

Which ONE of the following risks is most likely to be significant for Company M?

- ○ The emergence of a low-cost competitor
- ○ New technology becomes available across the market
- ○ A new entrant who provides similar products at a lower price
- ○ An underlying increase in raw material and component prices

---

3.9 Company N sells active-wear to customers in one country via a combination of its own website, a network of out-of-town retail outlets and a number of third-party retailers. Products include clothing for a variety of sports. The company is successful in its market and its products sell consistently. Shareholders are considered risk averse but would like to see the company continue to create value while maintaining its position. The board is currently debating its strategy and has arrived at four separate options.

Which ONE of the following options is Company N most likely to adopt?

- ○ Develop a range of footwear for use in the construction industry
- ○ Increase its advertising spend and run a series of promotions for its existing products
- ○ Export its current products to neighbouring countries
- ○ Offer high-quality knitwear products to its existing customers

---

3.10 B is a bank that has decided to adopt a policy of streamlining its services and business processes to attract a younger market and improve its growth. Part of this strategy means that the bank will stop sending out paper copies of bank statements, insurance policies and credit card bills to customers and only make them available either on their website or via their app.

Which are the key stakeholders in this decision?

Select ALL that apply.

☐ Employees

☐ Customers

☐ Paper suppliers

☐ Shareholders

☐ Information team

3.11 The board of Company P has concluded that it needs to make a strategic decision for one of its products, X. Although X has been selling consistently for the last five years, other similar products now exist, and there has been some innovation in this market by competitors, as well as the rise of some new entrants.

What should the company's strategy be for product X?

○ Increase production

○ Spend more on marketing

○ Withdraw product immediately

○ Maintain current spend but innovate via research & development

---

3.12 Company T is a supermarket selling groceries and other household products across a national network of stores of varying size and location. In order to embrace the digital revolution, Company T has decided to adopt electronic point of sales (EPoS) technology and remove cash altogether from its stores.

Which ONE of the following risks is T most likely to be exposed to as a result of the introduction of cash-free stores?

○ Reduced sales

○ Increase in armed robberies

○ Longer waits at checkouts

○ Impact on reputation

3.13 Company B is a manufacturer of engineering components. The company imports many of its raw materials and uses specialist labour to create products that are sold globally. Company B resides in a region that is considering breaking away from the single economic and legal framework of member states that it has been part of for the last 40 years in order to become more independent. Company B's current region has its own currency. The board of Company B is considering the impact that this departure will have on the company.

Which of the following disruptions are most likely to affect Company B as a result of the region breaking away?

Select ALL that apply.

☐ New legislation

☐ New governance requirements for Company B

☐ Capital availability

☐ Availability of labour and materials

☐ Export limits on sales

☐ Currency risk

3.14 A company is about to launch a new product. The company has developed a scenario-planning model to estimate future sales using variables including possible sales prices, current market data on sales volumes of similar products, limited market research on the new product and an externally sourced independent expert's advice.

Which ONE of the following risks is most likely to be mitigated by this activity?

○ Overspend on research and development expenditure

○ Inaccuracies in the new product's marketing budget

○ Legal action from competitors claiming copyright infringement

○ Errors in estimating the likely production capacity required

---

3.15 A company is attempting to mitigate the risks from disruptions to its strategy caused by changes in legislation. One of the techniques that it is considering using is game theory.

Which ONE of the following statements correctly defines game theory in this context?

○ The organisation's strategy should consider the actions of its competitors as well as its own actions.

○ The organisation should consider a range of possible outcomes from current trends as part of its strategic analysis.

○ A panel of experts is used to speculate about future developments and consider possible responses.

○ Experts are approached in isolation and asked for their opinions on strategic questions.

3.16 **Which ONE of the following is NOT one of the pillars in the Basel III guidance on sound banking practice?**

- ○ Minimum capital amounts
- ○ Profitability assessment
- ○ Visibility of risks
- ○ Improved disclosures

3.17 Allegations of bribery and corruption have been made against a company based in Eastern Europe but which has agents that operate in the UK and the US.

Which of the following risks does the company face?

Select ALL that apply.

- ☐ Legal action from US and UK authorities
- ☐ Legal action from the authorities in its own country
- ☐ Adverse impact on share price
- ☐ Reputation risk

3.18 **Which ONE of the following statements best describes reputation risk?**

- ○ The risk of untruthful or misleading behaviour by one or more participants in a particular process
- ○ The risk that you are perceived differently as a result of the adverse consequences of another risk
- ○ The risk of not adhering to a set of moral principles
- ○ The risks from offering an inducement for someone to perform their actions improperly

---

3.19 Company V operates in the automobile industry and is legally required to demonstrate that its engine emissions meet certain minimum standards of cleanliness. During the previous decade, the company created software that made its engines perform differently whenever their emissions were being tested, leading to artificially enhanced ratings that met the required minimum standards. Once discovered, the fact that the company's engine emissions are no longer considered clean severely affected the company's reputation, impacted sales and damaged the value of its brand.

Which ONE of the following strategies is Company V most likely to have followed immediately in the wake of this scandal to manage its reputation risk?

- ○ Continue manufacturing vehicles and engines in the same way as before
- ○ Improve the cleanliness of engines so they meet the minimum cleanliness standards
- ○ Communicate their apologies to all stakeholders
- ○ Change the governance structure of the company to avoid similar scandals in future

---

3.20 Company A is an online retailer selling a wide variety of products across many different countries. It has pursued a cost leadership strategy allowing it to offer extremely competitive prices. It has also developed a digital infrastructure that includes sales via its website alongside supplier management and fulfilment systems in operation at its distribution centres. A's customer service is generally considered to be excellent. However, media reports in many countries have also suggested that A's employees suffer poor treatment in the workplace, which has pushed a number of consumers towards other retailers instead.

Which ONE of the following statements is MOST accurate when describing the impact that A's strategy has had on its reputation?

- ○ A is a low-cost online retailer that offers a wide range of products and great customer service.
- ○ A is only interested in making money, regardless of the impact on its workforce.
- ○ A is a terrible company to work for.
- ○ A should be more like its competitors who value their staff.

---

4 Governance Risk

4.1 **Which THREE of the following represent examples of good, effective corporate governance?**

- ☐ The recruitment of NEDs with experience outside the industry the organisation operates in
- ☐ Full disclosure of director remuneration
- ☐ Senior management focusing exclusively on objectives linked to bonus payments
- ☐ Low staff turnover
- ☐ A clear distinction between the roles of chair and chief executive officer

---

4.2 **Which ONE of the following statements identifies the primary or main function of NEDs?**

- ○ To ensure adequate internal controls
- ○ To prevent domination of the board by a single individual
- ○ To consider and safeguard the interests of shareholders
- ○ To consider and safeguard the interests of creditors

4.3 Many companies operate a series of board sub-committees responsible for supervising specific aspects of governance using NEDs. The names of four board sub-committees are shown below.

Match each sub-committee name with the correct description.

Audit [▼]

Remuneration [▼]

Risk [▼]

Nominations [▼]

Pull down list:

The Committee responsible for advising on executive director salary and other rewards for directors

The Committee responsible for overseeing how prepared the organisation is to respond to possible threats

The Committee responsible for recommending the appointments of new directors to the board

The Committee responsible for liaising with external audit, supervising internal audit and reviewing the annual accounts and internal controls

---

4.4 **In the context of corporate governance, 'the agency problem' mainly refers to:**

○ The reliance of NEDs on executive directors to present all relevant information

○ The reliance of shareholders on directors to run the company

○ The lack of unity among shareholders

○ The reliance of external auditors on the work of internal audit

---

4.5 **Which THREE of the following statements are factors that would contribute to an effective board of directors?**

☐ A Nominations Committee that oversees the appointment of new directors

☐ A wide range of backgrounds and experience across board members

☐ Director remuneration packages with 80% of remuneration linked directly to the achievement of current year financial targets

☐ A well-respected, strong CEO

4.6 Non-executive directors and executive directors each bring different viewpoints and skills to the board of directors. The views of non-executive directors are independent. Executive directors run the company day-to-day so have a deeper understanding of the company than non-executive directors.

Are each of the following statements concerning executive directors and non-executive directors TRUE or FALSE?

	True	False
The view of an individual non-executive director should always carry more weight than the view of an individual executive director.	☐	☐
The view of an individual executive director should always carry more weight than the view of an individual non-executive director.	☐	☐
When considering the make-up and balance of the board, the number and status of non-executive directors should be sufficient to ensure their views carry significant weight.	☐	☐

4.7 **Which of the following is LEAST likely to be carried out by an audit committee?**

- ○ Review of the adequacy of financial systems
- ○ Review of risk management
- ○ Review of succession planning within the organisation
- ○ One-off investigations

4.8 **Which of the following would NOT be regarded as good practice for the nomination committee?**

- ○ The nomination committee should consider the need to attract board members from a diversity of backgrounds.
- ○ The nomination committee should consist entirely of executive directors.
- ○ The nomination committee should regularly review the structure, size and composition of the board.
- ○ The nomination committee should consider whether non-executive directors are spending enough time on their duties.
- ○ The nomination committee should use an external search consultancy and open advertising when recruiting a chair.

4.9 **Which of the following is LEAST true when considering the independence of non-executive directors?**

- ○ They should have no shareholdings in the company
- ○ They should be appointed for specific terms
- ○ Their service should not be pensionable
- ○ They should not have been employees of the company over the last few years

---

4.10 **Which ONE of the following statements relating to the board of directors and shareholders of a listed company is TRUE?**

- ○ The shareholders act as an agent of the board and have access to more information than the board.
- ○ The shareholders act as an agent of the board and have access to less information than the board.
- ○ The board act as an agent of the shareholders and have access to less information than shareholders.
- ○ The board act as an agent of the shareholders and have access to more information than shareholders.

4.11 Instead of a single or unitary board structure, some countries use multi-tier board structures. A multi-tier structure has some disadvantages.

Which of the following describe valid disadvantages of a multi-tier structure?

Select ALL that apply.

- ☐ Narrower stakeholder representation
- ☐ More bureaucratic
- ☐ Less accountability
- ☐ Reduced independence from operational pressures
- ☐ Less opportunity for domination by a single individual

4.12 **Which ONE of the following statements describes a difference between corporate governance practice for a global charity organisation and corporate governance practice for a commercial listed company?**

- ○ A charity will place less emphasis on internal control.
- ○ The board of a charity is not concerned with financial objectives.
- ○ The board of a charity is not concerned with decisions relating to strategy.
- ○ A charity will have different reporting responsibilities and committee structure.

4.13 **Which of the following statements represents poor corporate governance?**

Select ALL that apply.

- ☐ A focus on short-term profitability rather than long-term profitability
- ☐ Senior managers being asked to provide explanations to external auditors
- ☐ A strong internal audit function
- ☐ A focus on long-term profitability rather than short-term profitability
- ☐ Domination of the board by a single individual

4.14 M recently retired from his position of Managing Director of TT Co, 50 years after founding the company. M has been succeeded as Managing Director by his eldest son. The board are keen to retain access to M's experience and expertise. To facilitate this, they have asked M to remain on the board, as an NED.

Which of the following issues are likely to reduce M's effectiveness as a NED?

Select ALL that apply.

- ☐ Lack of true independence
- ☐ Insufficient knowledge of shareholder interests
- ☐ Lack of a wider perspective
- ☐ Unwilling to listen to other points of view

4.15 **Which ONE of the following statements correctly states the main advantage of ensuring diversity at board level of an organisation?**

- ○ Compliance with equal opportunity legislation
- ○ Enables the board to better understand the environment and market
- ○ Demonstrates that non-financial goals are important to the organisation
- ○ Presents an image of the organisation as a good corporate citizen

---

4.16 **Which ONE of the following would normally NOT be one of the roles of the chair of a company?**

- ○ Ensuring the board receives accurate and timely information
- ○ Leading the induction programme for new directors
- ○ Being responsible for developing new investment initiatives
- ○ Facilitating board appraisal
- ○ Helping to promote understanding of the views of directors

---

4.17 Company J collects data from various digital sources to provide a big data analysis service for the sports industry. Its clients include football and rugby clubs as well as athletics and swimming coaches and it aims to support elite triathletes as well. Due to the increasing take-up of its services, the company urgently needs to expand and will soon pass the threshold in the country where it operates that requires the adoption of corporate governance best practice. J currently employs two NEDs who will be considered for the various committees that are expected to be formed. The company also has an internal audit team which is currently overseen by these NEDs. However, analysis of the company's financial performance is undertaken by the Finance Director as both of the NEDs are ex-Olympic athletes with no business experience. They do understand the industry and the technology used by J, having pioneered some of it during their own sports careers.

From the information above, which of the following statements about Company J's current corporate governance arrangements is correct?

Select ALL that apply.

- ☐ The company can satisfactorily appoint an audit committee from its existing employees.
- ☐ The company can satisfactorily operate an audit committee using its existing employees.
- ☐ The company can satisfactorily recommend the appointment of further directors using its existing employees.
- ☐ The company can satisfactorily oversee the internal audit function using its existing employees.
- ☐ The company can satisfactorily manage the relationship with its external auditors using its existing employees.

4.18 Corporate governance best practice generally requires the use of a remuneration or compensation committee to determine policy on executive remuneration and ensure executive packages are designed with the organisation's objectives in mind.

Which ONE of the following would be the most appropriate example of a suitable remuneration package for an executive director in a profit-making company?

- ○ Basic pay fixed for each day worked by the director in any given month
- ○ Basic pay and a bonus based on the current year's performance by the company
- ○ Basic pay and share options that vest in three years' time
- ○ Basic pay, pension, healthcare benefits and a company car

---

4.19 Company P is a listed retailer with a strong brand and a solid reputation for quality products and good customer service in a very competitive environment. Twelve months ago, the company's chair and most of its NEDs resigned, leaving the company's Chief Executive free to become Executive Chairman, leading both the board and the company. Since this change of leadership, the company has reduced its investment in research and development, changed its remuneration structure to reward executives on the basis of the company's annual profits and pledged to increase the company's dividends by 10% every year.

Which ONE of the following statements describes the MOST likely impact on the company's strategy from the governance arrangements described above?

- ○ The company has adopted a new risk appetite to become more of a risk seeker than in previous years.
- ○ The company has added value to its brand by improving its offering to customers.
- ○ The company has decided to focus on short-term growth to satisfy its directors.
- ○ The company has decided to focus on long-term growth to satisfy its shareholders.

4.20 Company F is a food manufacturer in a stable market that does not employ any non-executive directors as it believes them to be 'an expensive waste of time and money'. It has decided to set strategy based on the outcome of board discussions between the finance director, chief executive, operations director and chair. Each of these individuals is remunerated on the basis of a fixed salary and a bonus of up to 2% of their salary if the company's share price grows by 15% in any given year.

Which ONE of the following strategic risks is most likely to be present from the information presented above?

- ○ Strategy will be accepted on the basis of financial factors alone
- ○ The company will pursue a strategy of significant growth and expansion
- ○ The company will undertake research and development into alternative foods that may not sell
- ○ Directors will decide to pursue a risk-seeking strategy that could affect profits

---

5 Internal Control Systems

5.1 Controls should be designed with the aim of reducing the main risks that a company faces.

Match each financial risk below with an appropriate control mechanism.

Risks:

Deterioration in relationships with customers and suppliers

[▼]

Failure to receive income that is due to the organisation

[▼]

Deterioration in the value of assets

[▼]

Transactions being completed without adequate authorisation

[▼]

Pull down list:

Establishment of a credit control department
Maintenance of a list of approved signatories
Dealings with customers and suppliers are on the terms that have been agreed
Physical safeguards against theft or damage

5.2 M Co is an exclusive supermarket chain with shops in several cities. Regular inventory counts are undertaken. However, the directors are concerned that there are often significant differences between the physical inventory on hand and the amounts shown in inventory records.

Which of the following controls would reduce the differences?

Select ALL that apply.

- ☐ Store security staff to check employees' bags at random when they are leaving the shop
- ☐ All purchases of goods for resale to be ordered by the buying department at head office
- ☐ All selling prices to be set by head office
- ☐ All goods should carry electronic tags that trigger alarms at store exits unless the goods have been scanned through the EPOS terminals/tills
- ☐ Monthly independent inventory counts to be undertaken by staff from other shops or from head office, with the results compared to inventory records

---

5.3 **Which ONE of the following is NOT primarily designed to ensure proper recording of purchases?**

- ○ Comparison of supplier statements with purchase ledger balances
- ○ Review of allocation of expenditure
- ○ Comparison of goods received notes with purchase orders
- ○ Reconciliation of purchase ledger control account to purchase ledger balances

---

5.4 **Which ONE of the following controls would best ensure that all monies received are banked?**

- ○ Daily bankings
- ○ Comparison of bank paying-in slips with initial receipt records
- ○ The amounts received being listed when the post is opened
- ○ Issuing receipts for amounts received

5.5 **Which ONE of the following controls would be LEAST effective in ensuring money is available to the business when required?**

- ○ Cash flow forecasts
- ○ Arrangements with the bank if cash shortages arise
- ○ Contingency funds
- ○ Hedging policy statement

5.6 **Which ONE of the following controls should contribute to assurance that depreciation is not charged on fully depreciated assets?**

- ○ Regular physical inspections to note the condition and usage of assets
- ○ Prior authorisation of sales or scrapping of assets
- ○ A register of tangible non-current assets maintained and reconciled to results of physical inspections
- ○ A tangible non-current assets register containing cost and accumulated depreciation of each asset

---

5.7 J is the management accountant for an independent tile retailer. The retailer has ten outlets, each of which is treated as an investment centre. J, who is based at head office, has been asked to implement a scheme that rewards the store manager and staff of the best performing store each financial year.

Which of the performance measures below is MOST appropriate for this purpose?

- ○ Customer satisfaction rating
- ○ Gross profit margin
- ○ Net profit earned
- ○ ROCE

5.8 G started an exercise class business called Jump 10 years' ago with her two friends. They started with just a few clients but now the business has grown and they employ 150 people to teach classes around the area. Clients pay by monthly direct debit. G is thinking of introducing a control system.

Which of the following statements apply to the above scenario?

Select ALL that apply.

- ☐ A control system will assist in compliance with laws and regulations.
- ☐ There is little point in having a control system because the business is fulfilling its objectives.
- ☐ The introduction of a control system is overdue.
- ☐ A control system will be inappropriate because the employees are creative individuals.
- ☐ The introduction of a control system will change the way the business operates.

5.9 T has been appointed Branch Manager, managing a large branch of a national clothes retailer. T has been informed by head office that each branch is treated as a separate profit centre.

Which of the following will fall under T's remit?

Select ALL that apply.

- ☐ Grow branch revenue
- ☐ Control branch costs
- ☐ Expand the branch network
- ☐ Investment responsibilities

5.10 J Co operates a factory that produces furniture. The factory has a number of controls in place.

Select the control procedure from the pull down list below that would be most appropriate for each of the following control objectives.

Prevent staff from over claiming the number of hours worked

[▼]

Prevent overpaying of purchase ledger amounts

[▼]

Prevent theft of portable plant and equipment

[▼]

Pull down list:

CCTV coverage
Timesheets signed by supervisor
Confirmation of information by suppliers

5.11 B Co has instituted some new controls over its procurement system. One such control is that the company always invites tenders for the provision of goods and services.

Which of the following control objectives does that control answer?

Select ALL that apply.

- ☐ The business does not pay too much for goods and services.
- ☐ The business does not purchase goods and services from connected parties.
- ☐ The business has goods and services when it needs them.
- ☐ The business has a central database of suppliers.
- ☐ The business researches potential suppliers before contracting with them.

5.12 **Which ONE of the following is NOT a control designed to ensure that assets are safeguarded?**

- ○ A register of non-current assets
- ○ Dispatch notes of goods sent out
- ○ Inventory counts
- ○ Review of accounting records to see if expenditure on non-current assets has been included as capital expenditure.

5.13 The following statements relate to internal controls.

1 One of the objectives of an internal control system is to eliminate risk.

2 Internal controls should be designed to manage risks and provide reasonable assurance that organisations will fulfil their objectives.

Which of the statements are true?

○ Both statements are true.

○ Both statements are false.

○ Statement 1 is true and Statement 2 is false.

○ Statement 2 is true and Statement 1 is false.

5.14 **Which TWO of the following are the main benefits of an effective internal control system?**

☐ Reduced time required for the external audit

☐ Safeguard the shareholders' investment

☐ Manage and control business risk

☐ Maximise profitability

5.15 A computer repair business keeps a store of computer parts. The parts store is locked and only T has a key. T only issues parts when she receives a signed parts requisition from J. If a repairs engineer requires a part, they ask J to sign a parts requisition. All parts requisitions are charged to specific repair jobs. An inventory count is carried out every two weeks by P.

Are the following statements true or false?

		True	False
1	P exercises some supervision over the work of T	☐	☐
2	Any fraud involving parts theft would have to involve P	☐	☐

5.16 The Project Support Office (PSO) is a government agency that provides a service desk and project support service to other government departments. Generally, service desk queries are relatively simple and project support queries are more complex.

Senior management have decided to introduce the balanced scorecard to monitor PSO performance.

Identify any areas that the PSO balanced scorecard should address.

Select ALL that apply.

☐ A target measure stating the minimum number of incidents to be handled by each member of staff per month

☐ Customer satisfaction measures

☐ Group target measures rather than individual measures

☐ Target call resolution time

☐ Differentiate between simple and complex queries and measure these separately

---

5.17 **Exception reporting within a business is:**

- ○ Where reports on routine matters are prepared on an 'ad hoc' basis
- ○ The scrutiny of all data as a matter of course, save in exceptional circumstances
- ○ The reporting of exceptional events, outside the normal course of events
- ○ The analysis of those items where performance differs significantly from standard or budget

---

5.18 **Which ONE of the following is an example of a qualitative non-financial control?**

- ○ Standard costing system
- ○ Balanced scorecard
- ○ Strategic plan
- ○ Activity-based management

5.19 BMC manufacture motor vehicles. One business unit within BMC produces alloy wheels. These wheels are supplied to BMC and to other motor vehicle manufacturers. The gross margin on sales to other vehicle manufacturers averages 35%. Transfer prices for 'internal sales' are set annually by the BMC finance department. The transfer price for the upcoming year has been set at cost price, as this makes it easier to establish a realistic figure of the full cost of a BMC vehicle supplied with alloy wheels.

Are the following three statements TRUE or FALSE?

Unless the alloy wheel business unit is obligated to supply BMC they are likely to prioritise external sales.	▼
Unless appropriate adjustments are made, the planned approach will distort the financial performance of the alloy wheel business unit.	▼
It is not possible to set realistic financial performance targets to the alloy wheel business unit under these circumstances.	▼

Pull down list:

True
False

5.20 A government-run budgetary advisory service uses the balanced scorecard to monitor performance.

Which ONE of the following criteria is most closely linked to the 'customer' perspective for this organisation?

- ○ Whether the advice provided enabled customers to better manage their finances
- ○ Staff turnover
- ○ Identifying the processes which service staff must carry out efficiently and effectively in order to deliver meaningful, timely advice
- ○ The percentage of staff in the service that possess a recognised financial qualification

---

5.21 **Which of the following organisations would be most suited to application of the management accounting technique EVA?**

Select ALL that apply.

- ☐ A management consultancy
- ☐ A motor vehicle manufacturer
- ☐ A software development company
- ☐ A mobile phone manufacturer
- ☐ An accounting partnership
- ☐ A commercial printing company

5.22 **One important aim of a post-completion audit is to:**

- ○ Obtain sign-off on all documentation by the project sponsor
- ○ Appraise the performance of the project manager
- ○ Capture organisational learning and document it to ensure lessons are learnt
- ○ Close the budget codes to prevent future expenditure

5.23 **A project objective should:**

- ○ Describe how the project fits the organisation's overall strategy
- ○ Describe the overall aim of the project
- ○ Describe how the overall aim of the project will be achieved
- ○ Describe a specific, required project outcome

5.24 **Quality management, in the context of project management, should focus on:**

- ○ Ensuring the fitness for purpose of deliverables
- ○ Inspection and testing of deliverables
- ○ Ensuring professionally presented project reports
- ○ The post-completion audit

5.25 **Identify the main benefits of post-completion auditing from the list below.**

Select ALL that apply.

- ☐ Improved decision making
- ☐ Better researched projects
- ☐ Improved internal controls
- ☐ Highlight reasons for successful projects
- ☐ The process is quick and inexpensive

5.26 KT Co produce tables and chairs for use by children. The furniture is produced in the KT factory, which runs three manufacturing production lines. Senior management are concerned about levels of wastage in the factory, and as a result is looking to improve the control environment.

Which of the following actions demonstrate a good control environment?

Select ALL that apply.

- ☐ Monthly inspection of production lines by senior management
- ☐ The performance of production line managers is based on the volume of production
- ☐ Staff are trained on new equipment
- ☐ Daily production logs and failure rates are noted
- ☐ Senior management require weekly calibration of equipment
- ☐ The maintenance staff who conduct the weekly calibrations need not complete records but should report any serious problems

---

5.27 **In which project report or document would you expect to find a cost-benefit review?**

- ○ Post-completion audit report
- ○ Project status report
- ○ Completion report
- ○ Budget report
- ○ Project quality report

5.28 Company Z has invested over $2 million in 20 projects over the past eight years. The directors of Z are unsure whether the company has always received value for money from their investment in capital projects. They are considering introducing a system of post-completion audits.

Which of the following are true with regard to a post-completion audit?

Select ALL that apply.

- ☐ Post-completion audits could produce valuable insights.
- ☐ Post-completion audits will not prevent dysfunctional behaviour by project sponsors.
- ☐ Project sponsors should be held liable for all negative findings from post-completion audits.
- ☐ It may be difficult to introduce post-completion audits.
- ☐ Only those projects starting after the audit system was introduced should be audited.

5.29 **Which of the following are aims of the post-implementation review of a new information system?**

Select ALL that apply.

- ☐ To ensure the system is secure
- ☐ To ensure the system meets the needs of managers
- ☐ To ensure the system produces accurate information
- ☐ To establish the time taken for the project
- ☐ To establish the costs incurred on the project

5.30 **Which ONE of the following represents an example of the fundamental ethical principle of professional competence and due care?**

- ○ Refusing to take on work where there is a conflict of interest
- ○ Raising concerns when asked to perform a specialised task outside your expertise
- ○ Maintaining confidentiality of sensitive information
- ○ Accepting responsibility for errors made

5.31 **Which of the following is LEAST likely to create a self-interest threat to a chief accountant employed by a listed company?**

- ○ Earning a $150,000 salary
- ○ Being entitled to share options currently worth $150,000
- ○ Owning shares currently worth $150,000
- ○ Being entitled to a $150,000 bonus if profits exceed a certain level

---

5.32 **Which of the following is least likely to result in an accountant breaching the requirement to act with professional competence and due care?**

- ○ Limited time to complete an assignment
- ○ Lack of information about an assignment
- ○ Lack of a superior to consult about problems with an assignment
- ○ Lack of a proper job description when the accountant was recruited

---

5.33 There are many situations that could cause ethical conflicts for an accountant working in practice, particularly in an audit role, threatening compliance with the fundamental principles.

Indicate what type of threat to the fundamental principles each of the following examples represents.

F has threatened to sack its auditors following a disagreement over the value of inventory in the financial statements.	▼
An audit partner has written a letter from his firm to his local paper, setting out a client's case in a lawsuit.	▼
Financial statements prepared by the Small Business Services department of T & B, an audit firm, are due to be audited by another T & B department.	▼
An audit partner has recently bought a large number of shares in a client company.	▼
The manager of the audit of C plc is the brother of C's finance director.	▼

Pull down list:

Self-interest
Intimidation
Familiarity
Advocacy
Self-review

6 Risk Management and Internal Control

6.1 The following are examples of internal controls and control activities which operate at JPN Co.

Match the following internal controls with the related control activity.

Authorisation ▼

Information processing ▼

Performance review ▼

Physical controls ▼

Segregation of duties ▼

Pull down list:

Changes to company IT applications can only be made by authorised system administrators.

The finance department compares actual quarterly results against budget.

The bank reconciliation is performed by the financial manager and all banking is done by the accounts clerk.

All overtime worked on production is approved by the production manager.

Access to the computer servers is restricted to IT department staff using a system of key cards.

6.2 **Match each of the control activities below to the correct type of control.**

A member of staff checks invoices from suppliers against goods received notes before they are paid.

[▼]

The credit controller chases customers who have exceeded their credit period.

[▼]

All customer services staff are given training and a procedures manual.

[▼]

Pull down list:

Prevent
Detect
Correct
Direct

6.3 **Which ONE of the following controls is not designed to prevent goods being supplied to a poor credit risk?**

○ Obtaining references for new customers

○ Regular review of customer payment records

○ Sequential numbering of blank order forms

○ Checks on customer files before an order is accepted to ensure there are no credit problems

---

6.4 CT Co manufactures and sells several types of tyre. The tyres are stored in a secure warehouse. An inventory count is carried out every quarter by warehouse staff and checked by the warehouse supervisor. Inventory sheets are filled in using pencil. Tyres are counted twice by two separate teams.

Which of the following risks arise as a result of CT Co's procedure?

Select ALL that apply.

☐ Collusion and misappropriation of inventory

☐ Error in the count

☐ Failure to make a permanent record of inventory

☐ Deterioration of inventory

6.5 Organisations exercise control over the individuals they employ.

Which ONE of the following statements regarding controls over employees is FALSE?

○ HR controls are more likely to be weak in a smaller business.

○ Employment contracts are a form of HR control.

○ The main reason control is exercised over employees is to prevent fraud.

○ The main reason control is exercised over employees is to ensure that their work contributes to achievement of the organisation's goals.

6.6 Teeming and lading is a fraud risk. It involves the misallocation of receipts to cover up missing funds that have been fraudulently removed from the business.

Poor segregation of duties between which of the following areas would increase the risk of this type of fraud occurring?

- ○ Stores department and goods outwards
- ○ Wages department and cash department
- ○ Receivables ledger and cash receipts
- ○ Payables ledger and goods inwards

6.7 M Co employs consultants who are based in remote locations around the world. S, a senior consultant based in a remote location, requested a team of four junior staff and recommended four suitable candidates. The four candidates were immediately employed by M Co, with the human resources department at head office taking care of the administration and paperwork. Because of S's recommendation, none of the usual background checks were performed. Since starting work, the four staff have submitted significant overtime and expense claims to S, who has authorised and passed them to payroll for payment.

Based on the scenario, which of the following are probable flaws in M Co's system?

Select ALL that apply.

- ☐ Insufficient checks on the need for additional staff
- ☐ Insufficient checks on employee identification, qualifications and background
- ☐ Lack of segregation of duties between overtime authorisation and payment
- ☐ Lack of staff training
- ☐ Insufficient control over the overtime approval process

6.8 HM Co manufacture automotive components. Orders for materials are made by department heads and signed by the production director. Only preferred suppliers are used. HM operate Just in Time (JiT) production. Goods delivered are received and used immediately without being checked. Invoices are paid on time by direct debit without reference to the original orders.

Which of the following are likely consequences of the HM Co system?

Select ALL that apply.

- ☐ False invoices could be paid
- ☐ Materials received could be stolen goods
- ☐ Inferior quality goods could be accepted
- ☐ The accounting value of materials in inventory stores could be incorrect

---

6.9 H works as a store manager for a large coffee shop chain. Over half of H's remuneration is dependent upon the store achieving monthly sales targets.

H is under pressure, which has resulted in dysfunctional behaviour.

Select from the options provided to classify the following examples of H's dysfunctional behaviour.

Opening 24 hours a day, 7 days a week, with H working many 12-hour shifts himself. As a consequence, customer service levels have suffered.

[▼]

Including the first day of the following month's trading in the previous month.

[▼]

Offering unsustainable 'bargain prices' to entice customers away from competitor shops.

[▼]

Pull down list:

Myopia
Tunnel vision
Misrepresentation

6.10 FPR Company has three divisions.

The Fruit Division (F) grows fruit (apples and oranges) for use in the production of fruit juice. F sells 75% of its fruit to FPR's Production Division (P) and sells the other 25% on the open market.

The P Division receives fruit from the F Division, inspects for quality and sends 'passed' fruit to the production line. The output of the line is juice packed in cartons.

P sells 100% of their production to FPR's Retail Division (R). The R Division sells the cartons of juice direct to the general public. All of the juice sold by R is sourced from P.

The three divisions are profit centres, and FPR uses return on investment (ROI) to assess divisional performance. Each division uses cost plus pricing for external sales and for internal transfers between divisions.

Three behavioural consequences that might arise as a result of the policy for the structure and performance evaluation of the divisions are shown below.

Match them to the correct division.

Note: A single division may be represented more than once.

	Division R	Division P	Division F
(a) Transfer costs may mean that profit and ROI is low and frustration will arise as they do not have a wide enough product range.	☐	☐	☐
(b) The main emphasis should be on technical efficiency and quality. ROI may conflict with these aims and the division may not replace machinery as it could worsen ROI.	☐	☐	☐
(c) This division must work closely with the other two divisions and being a profit centre may not be the best option.	☐	☐	☐

6.11 A very useful approach for a business to decide what information it should report on is to specify the business's critical success factors (CSF). Performance indicators are then specified for each CSF and the Management Information System (MIS) must be able to report in terms of these indicators.

Which THREE of the following would you suggest are used to measure the achievement of a retailer's CSF of offering excellent customer service?

- ○ Employee satisfaction scores
- ○ Number of returns
- ○ Queue lengths at tills
- ○ Customer satisfaction scores
- ○ Number of customer complaints

6.12 A doctor's practice is designing a new IT system to allocate patient appointments. Under the new system, the receptionist would ask patients seeking an appointment a series of questions and immediately input the answers into the IT system. The computer would use this information to make a recommendation to the receptionist. There are three possible recommendations: *Make appointment with doctor*; OR *Make appointment with nurse*; OR *No appointment required*.

A steering committee has been established to help ensure control during the design and implementation process.

Which of the following statements are true of a steering committee?

Select ALL that apply.

- ☐ The steering committee monitors the system implementation and the specific deliverables against the project plan. It has overall responsibility to ensure the system is delivered to the required time, cost and quality.
- ☐ The steering committee is responsible for creating the detailed budget for the new project.
- ☐ The steering committee brings together the sponsor of the project, the project manager who is responsible for the day-to-day delivery of the project, specialist IT staff with responsibility for delivering the project and user representatives with responsibility for accepting the system.
- ☐ The steering committee should also consider the detailed needs of the internal auditors.
- ☐ The steering committee should consider the ethical implications of the project.

6.13 **The term 'Big Data' refers to which of the following?**

1 Large volumes of structured data.
2 Large volumes of unstructured data.
3 The technology and techniques used to analyse that data.

- ○ 1 and 2
- ○ 2 and 3
- ○ 1 and 3
- ○ 1, 2 and 3

6.14 **Two statements relevant to Big Data follow. Are the statements TRUE or FALSE?**

1 Big Data analytics cannot be performed on complex, unstructured data.

2 Big Data analytics are now possible because of the amount of data storage that is available.

○ Both statements are true.

○ Statement 1 is true but Statement 2 is false.

○ Statement 1 is false but Statement 2 is true.

○ Both statements are false.

6.15 **A situation where data is run on both old and new systems for a specified time is an example of:**

○ Parallel running

○ Restricted data running

○ Pilot operation

○ Indirect changeover

6.16 **Which of the following would usually be done at the systems implementation stage?**

Select ALL that apply.

☐ Prototyping

☐ Training

☐ Testing

☐ Conversion

☐ Data flow diagrams

6.17 Company P is a wholesale and distribution company which currently services its customers from a central warehouse. The company has decided to computerise its stock control, order processing and sales accounting procedures, which have previously been executed manually. At the same time the company wishes to close its central warehouse as soon as possible and establish four regional distribution centres, linked to a central mainframe computer in a multi-user system.

Which of the following options represents the most appropriate approach to changing its systems?

○ Parallel running

○ Phased implementation

○ Pilot operation

○ Direct changeover

6.18 You have been employed by an organisation to introduce controls over systems development and acquisition. Such controls were previously non-existent. You decide to take the following steps to remedy the situation.

Steps:

1 Draw up a strategy for future systems development.

2 Conduct a survey to estimate the size of the problem (eg incompatibility of different makes of computer).

3 Lay down organisation-wide standards, with the active support of senior management, for equipment and software acquisition.

4 Develop procedures to ensure that capital expenditure on information technology is authorised centrally.

Which of the following is the logical order in which you should proceed?

- ○ Steps 1, 2, 3, 4.
- ○ Steps 2, 3, 1, 4.
- ○ Steps 4, 2, 3, 1.
- ○ Steps 4, 3, 2, 1.

6.19 TS Co manufactures steel which it supplies to a large number of car manufacturers. The company have six furnaces, each of which operate 24 hours a day, 7 days a week, 365 days a year.

TS's systems manager believes the company's information systems are in need of an overhaul. At present, the company computer network only extends to administrative offices.

Customer orders are scheduled by a production manager who plans production on a daily worksheet (hand written). The worksheet is photocopied, and a copy collected at the start of each shift by the six furnace supervisors.

The systems manager has proposed a new system. This would expand the computer network to all TS sites. Information would flow from the production manager to the furnace supervisors. Information relating to workflow and the operation of the furnaces would be fed back to the production manager.

Which of the following best describes the systems manager's proposal?

- ○ The proposed upgrade does not support TS's strategic requirements because the company should be gathering external information concerning new types of steel and new markets.
- ○ The proposed upgrade does not support TS's strategic requirements because the nature of the product and its manufacturing does not require an elaborate system.
- ○ The proposed upgrade is an exciting opportunity for TS to modernise its systems and gather valuable information.
- ○ The proposed new system will hugely reduce the company's operating costs.

6.20 **Which of the following issues would you expect to be addressed as part of the service level agreement (SLA) connected with an outsourcing contract?**

Select ALL that apply.

- ☐ Contractual flexibility
- ☐ Exit route
- ☐ Number of staff employed
- ☐ Other organisations for which services are supplied
- ☐ Standard of service level required

6.21 **Which THREE of the following represent aspects of 'Big Data' that are significantly different to earlier approaches to data collection and analysis?**

- ☐ The volume of data
- ☐ The proportion of external data
- ☐ Data is more consistent in type and structure
- ☐ The proportion of unstructured data
- ☐ Data is in digital form

6.22 Company B is a large retailer and has been collecting personal data on its customers for many years. One customer is very concerned that the data being held about him could be misused: he also suspects that some of it is inaccurate.

What are B's responsibilities under data protection legislation?

Select ALL that apply.

- ☐ B needs to obtain consent to hold sensitive personal data.
- ☐ B can pass on personal data to any third parties who request and pay for it.
- ☐ B must supply an individual with a copy of the data held, if asked to do so.
- ☐ B should make corrections when told about inaccurate data that it holds.
- ☐ B can keep customer data for as long as it likes.

6.23 Budgets and budgetary control systems are often used to monitor and appraise the performance of business units or responsibility centres. In this context, the management writer Hopwood (1973) identified three types of manager.

Match each of the manager types named below with the correct description.

Assessed through a comparison against short-term financial targets

[▼]

Assessed through non-budgetary performance measures

[▼]

Focus on the organisation continuing to achieve its overall financial goals

[▼]

Pull down list:

Non-accounting focused
Profit conscious
Budget constrained

---

7 Internal Audit

7.1 Planning is essential to help ensure an effective audit.

Which of the below represent objectives of the audit planning process?

Select ALL that apply.

- ☐ To set out the audit objectives and the other priorities that apply
- ☐ To define how the audit evidence necessary to achieve the objectives will be achieved
- ☐ To perform data analysis to identify major weaknesses
- ☐ To identify the resources that will be needed and actually employed in audits
- ☐ To perform compliance tests

7.2 Benchmarking is sometimes used as an audit tool, for example during analytical review.

Which ONE of the following statements correctly identifies the use of benchmarking as part of an analytical review?

- ○ Implementing quality management to match competitor standards
- ○ The use of business process re-engineering to implement best practice
- ○ Seeking external accreditation for quality processes
- ○ Comparing financial and non-financial performance with other organisations

---

7.3 **Which of the following statements concerning internal audit's role in risk management are true?**

1 Internal audit's primary role in a company is identifying risks.
2 Internal audit has a key role in determining company strategy to minimise risks.
3 Internal audit monitors risk strategies to ensure that they operate effectively.

- O 1 only.
- O 1 and 2 only.
- O 3 only.
- O 1, 2 and 3.

7.4 **Which ONE of the following is the best description of a management audit?**

- O It assesses the financial performance of the departments for which managers are responsible.
- O It is an audit by managers of their own departments.
- O It assesses whether adequate resources are being devoted to management and control.
- O It aims to reveal weaknesses in the performance of individual managers and in the overall management structure.

7.5 **Which of the following are primary objectives of tests of controls for internal auditors?**

Select ALL that apply.

- O Identify those persons within the organisation whose performance is not acceptable.
- O Establish whether the controls are operating as they are expected to be.
- O Establish whether the documentation relating to controls fairly reflects the operation of the system.
- O Establish whether improvements need to be made to controls.
- O Form an opinion as to the adequacy of the system as a whole for managing the risks identified.

7.6 The internal audit team of the B supermarket chain are auditing head office, focusing on staff recruitment.

B's recruitment procedures require all degree qualifications to be verified by B human resources staff before the new employee starts. An internal auditor has established that one employee, who started working in the marketing department three months ago, has not had their degree verified. The internal auditor has checked all head office employees and this employee is the only one with a degree that has not been verified.

How should the internal auditor proceed?

- O Consider the failure in light of the findings from investigation as a whole before deciding whether to report an adverse finding.
- O Flag this as a compliance error because part of the purpose of an internal audit is to encourage the application of procedures.
- O Report the compliance error to demonstrate a thorough audit has been performed.
- O Review the quality of the employee's work with a view to overlooking the failure on the grounds that the employee must be qualified if the work is satisfactory.

7.7 J works as an internal auditor for a company that uses standard costs for budgeting and to produce monthly variance reports. The system operates as follows:

(i) Variances are reported to the managers responsible within three working days of the end of each month.

(ii) Managers are required to investigate variances in excess of 10% of standard cost.

(iii) Managers are required to report to their superior, in writing, on the reasons for variances and the control measures implemented to reduce future variances, within one week of receiving the report.

J is carrying out an audit of the budgetary control system in one of the company's operating centres.

Which of the following are compliance tests?

Select ALL that apply.

☐ Establish the details of the standard costing and budgetary system. Find out how costs are recorded and how variances are produced and distributed at month end.

☐ Check whether variances are reported within three working days of month end.

☐ Check whether the 10% figure for exceptional variances is reasonable.

☐ Suggest improvements to the system.

☐ Check whether managers report reasons for variances and control action taken within one week.

☐ Perform detailed tests to establish how staff report variances to managers.

7.8 **Select the correct option to complete the sentence below.**

To be effective, internal audit should work [▼] other areas of the organisation.

Pull down list:

Collaboratively with
Independent of
Integrated with
Subordinately to

7.9 Analytical procedures are a powerful tool for both internal and external auditors.

Which ONE of the following statements is NOT true in respect of analytical procedures used by internal auditors?

○ Analytical procedures may be used as substantive procedures.

○ Analytical procedures are often used as tests of controls.

○ Analytical procedures can be used in certain circumstances as an alternative to detailed testing of transactions and balances.

○ Analytical procedures can be used as part of risk assessment to highlight areas in which further work may be required.

○ Analytical procedures are often used as a final review procedure.

7.10 **Which ONE of the following audit tests would provide evidence that sales had been completely recorded?**

- ○ Testing the sequence of dispatch notes and enquiring into any missing items
- ○ Reviewing sales ledger accounts of individual customers
- ○ Checking that statements are sent out regularly to customers
- ○ Checking items in the sales ledger to the sales day book

7.11 **A review of the revenues and expenses in the detailed statement of profit or loss and other comprehensive income of a company, involving investigation of significant variations in comparison with the equivalent figures for the previous year, is most likely to detect which of the following significant problems?**

- ○ The fact that a line of inventory has become obsolete during the year and should be written off
- ○ A misallocation of distribution costs as advertising expenses
- ○ The fact that the costs of some exceptional repairs to the company's premises have not been included in the statement of profit or loss
- ○ Failure to make a provision for volume discounts which have been introduced this year for major customers

---

7.12 As new auditor of Company L, you note that the company's gross profit percentage as per the draft financial statements has fallen from 30% in the previous year to 20% in the current year.

Which of the following explanations do you consider to be the MOST plausible?

- ○ Errors in computation have caused opening inventory to be undervalued and this has been compounded by the inclusion for the first time (so as to comply with IAS 2 *Inventories*) of indirect overheads in the closing inventory valuation.
- ○ Errors in computation led to opening inventory being overvalued and the company has also increased sales as a result of a marketing drive based on undercutting competitors.
- ○ Errors in computation led to the opening inventory being overvalued and this has been compounded by the inclusion for the first time (so as to comply with IAS 2 *Inventories*) of indirect overheads in the closing inventory valuation.
- ○ Errors in computation led to opening inventory being undervalued and margins have fallen as a result of the entry into the market of a major new competitor.

7.13 The receivable days figure in a manufacturing company has increased from 30 days to 60 days.

Which of the following explanations may have caused this rise?

Select ALL that apply.

- ☐ Customers are paying more promptly than they used to.
- ☐ Customers are taking longer to pay than they used to.
- ☐ Credit terms to receivables have changed.
- ☐ The accounting records on which the calculation has been based may be inaccurate.
- ☐ Cash received from customers may have been misappropriated.

7.14 Company P is concerned about the independence of its internal audit function.

Which of the following would help ensure independence?

Select ALL that apply.

☐ Outsource the internal audit function.

☐ Ensure the Head of Internal Audit has access to the Chair of the Board of Directors and is accountable to the Audit Committee.

☐ Ensure the internal auditors are physically separate from the rest of the workforce.

☐ Ensure the internal auditors work closely with the executive directors.

☐ Ensure all internal auditors have previously worked in another area of P to enable them to provide insight and understanding.

7.15 **Which ONE of the following audit tests would not be relevant in testing procurement?**

○ Reviewing a sample of contracts to confirm supplier was selected after thorough research and tender procedure

○ Reviewing suppliers to confirm that none appear to be connected with employees

○ Checking movements of inventory from one of the organisation's locations to another

○ Comparing invoices with original purchase requisitions

7.16 **Which ONE of the following audit procedures is a test of controls?**

○ Checking that the total shown on the aged list of receivables has been correctly analysed

○ Checking that approved sales orders indicate that reference was made to the aged listing

○ Checking that the aged listing has used as a basis for credit control decisions

○ Checking that the total of the nominal ledger receivables control account agrees to the total shown by the aged listing

---

7.17 **What is the main advantage in using statistical sampling in auditing?**

○ To reduce the need for audit judgement

○ To ensure that a representative sample is selected

○ To reduce the number of items to be tested

○ To provide an objective estimate of the probability of error in the population

---

7.18 You work within the internal audit department of a soft drinks manufacturer that operates a divisional structure across 12 sites in three countries. Products are distributed across the rest of the world via a number of third-party sales agents who are remunerated on a 'step fixed price' contract basis that is flexed when certain sales volumes are achieved. Cost control is key to success as the products sold are price-sensitive and ingredients can vary in quality as well as price. Each of the products sold is differentiated from other similar drinks in the same industry due its high-quality brand image: as a consequence, the company has very little competition due to its enduring demand in the eyes of consumers.

Which of the following procedures completed by the internal audit department would indicate that the team was prioritising its activities effectively?

Select ALL that apply.

- ☐ Analysis of revenue by country
- ☐ Analysis of gross operating margins by manufacturing site
- ☐ Analysis of wastage by site
- ☐ Advising the production team about the standards used in the company's costing system
- ☐ Verifying volumes delivered by each sales agent

7.19 As part of their responsibilities, internal auditors may perform fraud investigations.

Which of the following represent the conditions necessary for fraud to occur?

Select ALL that apply.

- ☐ Collusion
- ☐ Rationalisation
- ☐ Opportunity
- ☐ Pressure
- ☐ Complacency

7.20 **Which of the following controls is designed to guard against ghost employees - imaginary employees being paid wages or salaries?**

Select ALL that apply.

- ☐ Review of the number of employees required to achieve a certain amount of work
- ☐ Requiring employees being paid cash wages to collect them in person
- ☐ Recording of hours worked by timesheets
- ☐ Comparison of payroll with employee personnel records

7.21 **Which of the following tasks could internal audit appropriately carry out when reviewing the work of the treasury function?**

Select ALL that apply.

- ☐ Checking operations on a day-to-day basis
- ☐ Approving the size and nature of transactions
- ☐ Checking the adequacy of contingency arrangements
- ☐ Reviewing forecasts of future activities

---

8 Cybersecurity Threats

8.1 **Which of the following types of information is MOST susceptible to cybersecurity risk due to its sensitivity?**

Select ALL that apply.

- ☐ Customer names
- ☐ Employee ethnic origin
- ☐ Company bank details
- ☐ Company bank statements
- ☐ Employee emails
- ☐ Company phone numbers

8.2 Company X is determining what its cybersecurity objectives should be for a variety of areas of its operations. One of the draft objectives states that information should be accessible, but only to those with the right to have it, for legitimate purposes only.

Which of the following categories does this objective refer to?

- ○ Availability
- ○ Confidentiality
- ○ Integrity of data
- ○ Integrity of processing

8.3 When considering how to combat the threat of social engineering, cybersecurity controls may discuss some of the ways that people are influenced, based on the work of Robert Cialdini.

From the following list, which of the following are recognised influences from Cialdini's work?

Select ALL that apply.

- ○ Imitation
- ○ Social proof
- ○ Authority
- ○ Reciprocation
- ○ Plausibility

8.4 Company Y is a clothing manufacturer and retailer and is determining the process it should use for establishing, maintaining and approving its cybersecurity objectives for the first time. Currently, the process is expected to be a formal part of the board's overall objectives and is to be considered on an annual basis.

Which ONE of the following additional elements is this process MOST likely to include?

- ○ External expertise on cybersecurity
- ○ Budgets for implementation
- ○ Appointment of a chief information officer
- ○ Benchmarking with other similar organisations

8.5 Company X is a retailer that sells products using its own website. It has no other sales channels. It holds inventory in warehouses and dispatches orders from the same location. Inventory levels are monitored by suppliers and automatically replenished when they reach a certain threshold.

Which TWO of the following technologies and delivery channels will Company X use as part of its retail operations?

- ☐ Internet
- ☐ Intranet
- ☐ Website
- ☐ Phone
- ☐ Social media

8.6 Company Y sells fuel to drivers of all types of vehicles. Fuel is sold from roadside service stations which have a distinctive logo that drivers can see from the road. Service stations are also advertised by road signs located further up the road that indicate their location. Customers can only use cash to pay for their fuel. Each service station records its sales using a PC that creates a daily printout of fuel dispensed and cash taken for each transaction. The price of fuel is emailed to each service station at the start of each week. Printouts are sent in the post to head office for entry into a manual ledger system.

Which ONE of the following statements best describes the cybersecurity threat posed to Company Y from its current technology and delivery channels?

- ○ Company Y faces no cybersecurity threats.
- ○ Company Y faces cybersecurity threats from both its technology and its delivery channels.
- ○ Company Y faces cybersecurity threats from its technology only.
- ○ Company Y faces cybersecurity threats from its delivery channels only.

8.7 A change in government has led to the introduction of online learning resources for all school children, including a virtual learning environment (VLE) and an individual email account for each child. Email and the VLE are both accessible via each child's own device, which is supplied by the government. Children are encouraged to use the internet for research purposes as part of their studies. Once they have completed an assessment, children email them to their local school for marking from their individual email account.

Which ONE of the following cybersecurity risks will schools be exposed to as a result of this new policy?

- ○ Viruses
- ○ Hacking
- ○ Ransomware
- ○ Phishing

8.8 Company T is an engineering company which is experiencing financial problems and has seen reducing profits over recent years. To address this, the company decides to stop spending any more money on its cybersecurity and make do with its existing technology.

Which of the following risks will the company be exposed to as a result of this new policy?

Select ALL that apply.

- ☐ Financial
- ☐ Reputation
- ☐ Legal
- ☐ Commercial
- ☐ Social

8.9 An oil and gas pipeline company uses a digital control system (DCS) to manage the flow of oil and gas throughout its network in order to meet customer demand and allow safe usage of its pipelines. The DCS allows company management to control the valves within the network to allow individual pipelines to either open or close from a central point. This is currently controlled via a network of sensors attached to telecommunication cables that connect each pipeline to the central point. The company is responsible for ensuring that valves do not create environmental hazards by opening when they should remain closed. Pipelines are frequently damaged by environmental conditions, as is also the cabling used by the DCS, but the company only knows about this when the DCS issues a warning signal.

Which ONE of the following changes will have the most significant effect on the company's cybersecurity risk management program?

- ○ Replacing the network cables with wireless technology to maintain contact with each sensor
- ○ Screening all new employees with access to the DCS for links to terrorist organisations
- ○ Introducing a planned maintenance programme for inspecting pipelines, sensors and cables
- ○ Increasing the frequency that the DCS anti-virus software is updated from monthly to weekly

---

8.10 Phishing is a cybersecurity term used to describe the theft of login details, credit card numbers or passwords for personal gain. There are many different types of phishing that can occur.

Match the following terms with the correct definition from the dropdown boxes.

Spear phishing	▼
Smishing	▼
Vishing	▼

Pull down list:

Disabling a system by bombarding it with more activity than it can cope with
Extorting money by blocking access to files or systems until a fee is paid
Targeting an individual instead of an entire population
The use of telephone calls
Using text messages

8.11 Company Q has decided to outsource its IT support function to an external provider, including monitoring of its cybersecurity threats. This monitoring was previously carried out by staff employed by Company Q. As a result of this decision, a number of the company's IT staff were made redundant but some have now been employed by the outsourcing provider on a part-time basis to provide a cybersecurity risk management programme. The rest have left the company under a voluntary redundancy (VR) scheme.

Which ONE of the following risks is the company MOST exposed to as a direct result of the decision to outsource its IT function?

- ○ Reputation risk
- ○ Cybersecurity risk
- ○ Financial risk
- ○ Litigation risk

8.12 A university operates from one campus location. There are two separate wireless networks in place on this campus: an unsecured public system for students to access their virtual learning environment (VLE), websites and social media as well as submitting work via email to their tutors for assessment; and a more secure private system that is used by tutors and other staff to access the university's network and other online resources. Visitors and contractors working on the campus are given access to the public system if they need to go online during their time on campus.

Which of the following cybersecurity threats to the university's private network are created by the university's current wireless network arrangements?

Select ALL that apply.

- ☐ Malware from students
- ☐ Malware from visitors to the campus
- ☐ Malware from hackers
- ☐ Malware from non-teaching staff

8.13 **Which of the following would be considered an internal threat arising from malware?**

Select ALL that apply.

- ☐ Ransomware
- ☐ Hacking
- ☐ Unauthorised websites accessed by staff
- ☐ Illegally obtained software
- ☐ Infected memory sticks
- ☐ Employees with a grudge against the organisation
- ☐ Spyware

8.14 **Which of the following would be a suitable defence against cybersecurity threats arising from hacking?**

Select ALL that apply.

- ☐ Monitoring software
- ☐ Taking legal action against all offenders
- ☐ Appointing an information officer
- ☐ Contingency planning
- ☐ Firewalls

8.15 Company K has suffered a cybersecurity breach from a web application attack where its servers have been illegally accessed and confidential personal data from customers obtained.

Which ONE of the following terms does this description relate to?

- ○ Hacking
- ○ Ransomware
- ○ Phishing
- ○ Distributed denial of service attack

8.16 There are many different types of web application attacks that an organisation might be exposed to when operating online. One of these could be a cross-site scripting (XSS) attack.

Which ONE of the following terms is the best description of this particular type of cyber-attack?

- ○ Where data can be accessed via legitimate access to a company's website
- ○ An attack which uses an innocent third party's website to host a cyber-attack
- ○ Where a system is bombarded with more data than it can handle
- ○ Where access to data is restricted unless some form of payment is made to the cyber-attacker

---

8.17 **Which of the following would be appropriate defences against a web application attack such as ransomware or distributed denial of service attack?**

Select ALL that apply.

- ☐ Appointing a chief information officer
- ☐ Anti-virus software
- ☐ Filters against malware
- ☐ User education
- ☐ Threat-monitoring software
- ☐ Cybersecurity risk assessment

8.18 **Which ONE of the following is a cybersecurity threat created by unethical hackers?**

- ○ Exploiting gaps in cybersecurity for their own purposes
- ○ Identifying gaps in cybersecurity so they can be addressed before they create a threat
- ○ Exploiting someone's trust to gain illegal access to personal data
- ○ Offering to fix a cybersecurity threat for a fee or posting the weakness online if the offer is not taken up

---

8.19 **Which ONE of the following is a cybersecurity threat created by grey hat hackers?**

- ○ Exploiting gaps in cybersecurity for their own purposes
- ○ Identifying gaps in cybersecurity so they can be addressed before they create a threat
- ○ Exploiting someone's trust to gain illegal access to personal data
- ○ Offering to fix a cybersecurity threat for a fee or posting the weakness online if the offer is not taken up

---

8.20 Company X is a private publishing company which sells books in both hard copy and soft copy (ie for use by electronic readers). Company X experiences a cybersecurity breach where intellectual property (IP) is stolen and customer data is accessed.

Which of the following potential downside risks is Company X exposed to as a result of the cybersecurity breach?

Select ALL that apply.

- ☐ Opportunity cost from lost revenue
- ☐ Fines and penalties from data regulators
- ☐ Loss of share price
- ☐ Increased production costs

---

9 Cybersecurity Processes

9.1 An information system contingency plan or disaster recovery plan should provide for standby procedures, recovery procedures and personnel management.

Match the descriptions below to the correct aspect of a disaster recovery plan.

Procedures implemented after the cause of the breakdown has been discovered or corrected

[▼]

Procedures that ensure that some operations can be performed during the period that normal services are disrupted

[▼]

Policies to ensure that the recovery plan is implemented and operates as intended

[▼]

Pull down list:

Personnel
Recovery
Standby

9.2 F Co is a company which produces very expensive parts for ships and ferries. The parts are delivered all over the world. F Co has an excellent IT system which controls the ordering and delivery. The parts usually cost around $1 million to make and take about ten days to build. F Co has a disaster recovery site around 250 miles from head office, which is tested annually. It takes two days to activate but incurs minimal cost to maintain. F Co is now ready to refresh its entire IT infrastructure at a cost of $3 million. It does this every four years. Four options for the refresh of the disaster recovery plan are shown below.

Which ONE represents the best course of action for F Co?

- ○ Continue with its existing disaster recovery site and infrastructure, no additional cost
- ○ Re-use the infrastructure that will be replaced at the current disaster recovery location at a cost of $0.25 million
- ○ Install a new disaster recovery site more locally at a cost of $2.1 million
- ○ A second system should be installed at head office in case the first one fails

---

9.3 **Which THREE of the following should a disaster recovery plan provide for?**

- ☐ The use of firewalls
- ☐ Personnel management
- ☐ Standby procedures
- ☐ Physical access control
- ☐ Recovery procedures

9.4 **Which TWO of the following would be found in an organisation's cybersecurity risk governance structure?**

- ☐ Establishing, maintaining and communicating integrity and ethical values
- ☐ User training to identify cybersecurity threats
- ☐ Agreeing policy on cybersecurity suppliers
- ☐ Providing board oversight

9.5 Company A has implemented a cybersecurity program that uses externally purchased software and hardware in conjunction with a third-party data processing company and external cloud computing for data storage.

Which of the following techniques would Company A find most useful when identifying, assessing and managing the risks associated with its cybersecurity vendors and business partners?

Select ALL that apply.

- ☐ Having a sponsor at board level
- ☐ Service level agreements (SLAs)
- ☐ Key performance indicators (KPIs)
- ☐ Accreditation using ISO 27001
- ☐ Enter into partnership with another organisation

9.6 Company K is a manufacturer of components used in the telecommunications industry. One of its core suppliers is Company E, which operates mines to obtain a scarce metallic element used in K's components. During private negotiations to extend the supply contract between K and E, a rival mining company, G, has contacted K with detailed proposals to meet and exceed the levels of service currently proposed by E, along with a substantial reduction in price. Negotiations have been undertaken using emails that both K and E believe to be secure.

Which ONE of the following terms BEST describes the situation presented by this scenario?

- ☐ Phishing
- ☐ Man in the middle attack
- ☐ Social engineering
- ☐ Malvertising

9.7 Company E has developed a cybersecurity policy to include objectives, expectations, responsibilities and related matters which it needs to communicate to both internal and external users of this policy. This includes its legal responsibilities as part of recently introduced legislation designed to secure any personal data collected and stored during normal business activities.

Which ONE of the following techniques would be the MOST appropriate technique for Company E to educate internal users?

- ○ Intranet
- ○ Service level agreement (SLA)
- ○ Liaison officers
- ○ Contracts

9.8 As part of their cybersecurity policies, organisations need to have suitable preventive and detective controls in place against certain vulnerabilities. Company H uses a combination of anti-virus software, user education, a 'bring your own device' policy and a firewall to manage one particular cybersecurity vulnerability.

From the list below, select the most appropriate vulnerability that the controls in place in Company H are designed to address.

○ Malware

○ Sensitive data being intercepted

○ Social engineering

○ Loss of data due to natural disaster

9.9 Company M is in the process of developing a policy that addresses disaster planning: specifically, what happens if the organisation is experiencing a disaster such as fire, flood or earthquake that affects its ability to operate.

Which of the following would you expect to see in this kind of disaster plan?

Select ALL that apply.

☐ List of responsible staff

☐ Budget allocations

☐ Business continuity arrangements

☐ Communications protocols

☐ Insurance details

9.10 Blockchain and distributable ledgers are used to conduct business online and operate using secure and centralised records of activity for all parties in the blockchain to make them transparent and authoritative. They rely on a specific type of cybersecurity technique to ensure these records cannot be manipulated.

Which ONE of the following terms BEST describes the cybersecurity technique used in blockchain technology?

☐ Patch management

☐ Firewall

☐ Back-up

☐ Encryption

9.11 As part of the process for developing suitable responses to assessed cybersecurity risks, a small company is implementing control processes that relate to its software and network controls.

Which TWO of the following will be relevant controls to address these risks?

☐ Recruitment of an information officer

☐ Introducing secure cloud computing for all data storage

☐ Controls that preserve data and systems integrity

☐ Purchasing legitimate software from reputable suppliers

9.12 Consider the following job description from an employee of an organisation.

> I work within a part of the business that is responsible for cybersecurity. We monitor data activity for patterns which could indicate cybersecurity threats. Other teams are employed to act on the intelligence created by my team.

Which ONE of the following terms BEST describes the part of the business where this employee works?

- ○ Insider threat team
- ○ Threat intelligence team
- ○ Hunt team
- ○ Incident response team
- ○ Security information and event management

9.13 An organisation is looking to obtain certification as ISO 27001 compliant and has recruited an expert to manage the process of achieving accreditation for its cybersecurity responses.

Which of the following elements would be included in an ISO 27001 accreditation process?

Select ALL that apply.

- ☐ Demonstrate compliance with the General Data Protection Regulation (GDPR)
- ☐ Apply consistent methodology for cybersecurity across the organisation
- ☐ Apply TARA approach to determine how to manage risks
- ☐ Assessment of statement of applicability by accredited auditor
- ☐ Obtain assurance for customers that cybersecurity is effective

---

9.14 An organisation is looking to implement ISO 27001 accredited responses to manage its cybersecurity threats.

Which ONE of the following controls would you NOT expect to find within the ISO 27001 recommended control sets?

- ○ Human resources security (policies for staff)
- ○ Internal audit
- ○ Physical and environmental security
- ○ Systems development, acquisition and maintenance
- ○ Business continuity management

9.15 Y is a small, not-for-profit organisation run by a board of trustees in line with the legislation that operates in its home country. It employs 30 people, most of whom are involved in approaching members of the public to donate money on a regular basis via their bank accounts. It holds details of all its donors on a network that it operates at its head office.

Which ONE of the following best describes the process that Y should use to assess the effectiveness of its cybersecurity controls?

- ○ As a charity, Y is exempt from data protection legislation so has no need for cybersecurity
- ○ ISO 27001 accreditation by an external provider
- ○ The trustees will rely on the internal auditors' systems audit report
- ○ Y will focus on the chief information officer's report to the board of trustees

---

9.16 Company X has just learned that it recently experienced a cybersecurity breach where personal data from its staff and customers was hacked using a sophisticated malware never before seen. X operates an outsourced cybersecurity function provided by a third party.

Which ONE of the following suggestions represents the best corrective action that Company X should now take?

- ○ Inform regulators within 72 hours
- ○ Request suitable updates to its cybersecurity to stop the malware from affecting its systems
- ○ Take legal action against the outsourced cybersecurity function
- ○ Review the affected data subjects and inform them of the breach

---

9.17 **Which of the following items would you expect to see as outputs from a cybersecurity monitoring system following a specific event?**

Select ALL that apply.

- ☐ Reduction in share price
- ☐ Reputation risk
- ☐ Reports to board or senior management
- ☐ The requirement to inform data protection regulators
- ☐ Resignation of the risk manager

---

10 Cybersecurity Tools, Techniques and Reporting

10.1 Company G is a supplier of stationery goods to schools, universities and other educational establishments. It operates a website from which customers can order and pay for goods. It also uses an online e-commerce system to manage its suppliers. Company G has just identified a cybersecurity breach in its firewall and intends to use forensic analysis to investigate the breach.

Which ONE of the following statements BEST describes the use of forensic analysis by Company G to investigate the breach?

- ○ The analysis will determine the cause and extent of the breach by identifying the malware used.
- ○ The analysis will confirm the identity of the attackers who first created the malware used in the breach.
- ○ The analysis will identify the source and intent of the malware and determine the consequences of the breach.
- ○ The analysis will explain the way that the malware was used so the company can stop further breaches from occurring.

10.2 **Which ONE of the following terms best describes decompilation?**

- ○ Converting binary code into source code for the purposes of responding to a malware threat
- ○ Breaking binary code apart for the purposes of responding to a malware threat
- ○ Converting binary code into assembler code for the purposes of responding to a malware threat
- ○ Breaking binary code apart for the purposes of creating a malware threat

---

10.3 **Which of the following terms is NOT used to respond to known or potential malware threats?**

Select ALL that apply.

- ☐ Reverse engineering
- ☐ Social engineering
- ☐ Decompilation
- ☐ Disassembly
- ☐ Defragmentation

10.4 **Which ONE of the following statements BEST describes penetration testing?**

- ○ Probing a system as part of cybersecurity testing to expose vulnerabilities that can be addressed
- ○ Exploiting someone's trust to gain illegal access to personal data
- ○ Exploiting gaps in cybersecurity for your own purposes
- ○ Converting binary code into source code for the purposes of responding to a malware threat

---

10.5 **When would an organisation use penetration testing?**

- ○ To determine the cause, culprits and consequences of malware
- ○ Identifying gaps in cybersecurity so they can be addressed before they create a threat
- ○ As part of cybersecurity testing when looking for exploitable vulnerabilities
- ○ As part of a cyber risk reporting framework

10.6 **Which ONE of the following would be an appropriate security standard for software?**

- ○ SOC for cybersecurity
- ○ SOC 2
- ○ ISO 31000
- ○ BYOD policy

10.7 **Which of the following would the board of directors of a company be most likely to need to know as part of their organisation's cybersecurity risk reporting framework?**

Select ALL that apply.

- ☐ Leadership roles for cybersecurity
- ☐ Cybersecurity budgets
- ☐ Vendor due diligence
- ☐ Officers responsible for making cybersecurity decisions
- ☐ Feedback on cybersecurity events
- ☐ Links between cybersecurity objectives and organisational objectives

---

10.8 Company J has outsourced its payroll function to a third-party service organisation. The contract in place between the two organisations lists the key cybersecurity reporting needs of Company J when assessing the performance of the service organisation.

From the following options, which would you expect to find on a list of key cybersecurity reporting needs.

Select ALL that apply.

- ☐ Number of cybersecurity breaches in last six months
- ☐ Average time taken to process the payroll
- ☐ Benchmark data against other payroll providers
- ☐ Details of SOC 2 accreditation
- ☐ SOC for Cybersecurity accreditation

10.9 **Which of the following items would you expect to see in a SOC for cybersecurity report?**

Select ALL that apply.

- ☐ A description of the cybersecurity system used by management
- ☐ An assessment of the controls in a service organisation
- ☐ A list of the detailed tests carried out by the certified public accountant (CPA)
- ☐ Assertions made by management about the cybersecurity controls in place
- ☐ An opinion by a CPA that the controls in place were effective
- ☐ A list of the parties that can access the report

10.10 **Which of the following items would you expect to see in a SOC 2 report?**

Select ALL that apply.

- ☐ An opinion by a CPA that the description in the assertion matches the AICPA trust services criteria
- ☐ An opinion by a CPA that the controls in place were effective
- ☐ A description of the cybersecurity system used by management
- ☐ A statement that the criteria used are management's own
- ☐ Assertions made by service organisation management about the description of controls

---

Answers to objective test questions

1 Risk and Risk Exposure

1.1 The correct answer is: Machine failure risk increases and human error risk falls

Machine failure risk increasing and human error risk falling is a necessary trade off when introducing automation and is the most likely option here. Labour costs will fall not rise, and although the speed of manufacturing might rise with automation, it is being considered for quality purposes. Sales may improve as the company's reputation for better build quality spreads, but this may just be to restore market leadership as P is looking to maintain its position, not grow it.

1.2 The correct answer is: Statement 1 true; Statement 2 true

1.3 The correct answer is: Risk can recognise positive events, including opportunities.

Risk can include things that occur more favourably than expected.

1.4 The correct answer is: Risk analysis is about understanding the impact or severity of a risk or risks, as well as their probability or **likelihood**.

1.5 The correct answer is: A merger between the business's sole supplier of one component and the business's main competitor.

This is an example of a strategic risk because of the significance of the role played by both parties. The other risks are more likely to be operational in nature (the move to manufacture goods in a developing country might indicate 'sweatshop' connections that could have damaging strategic risks to reputation).

1.6 The correct answer is: Sensitivity analysis

Note. Value at risk is not numerically examinable in P3.

1.7 The correct answer is: Risk mapping

Risk mapping is a technique for assessing risks, in terms of frequency and severity. It leads on to risk measurement, but is not itself a technique for measuring risk. Risks can be measured as (severity × frequency) or (impact × probability), for which techniques such as statistical analysis (for example standard deviation and variance) and sensitivity analysis can be used.

1.8 The correct answer is: 218.5%

The expected value of cash flows for each year can be calculated as (60% × 800) + (40% × 300) = 600

The cumulative discount factor for 5 years at 12% = 3.605 while the 5-year 12% present value factor is 0.567

The project's NPV is therefore:

	$'000
Initial investment at T0	(2,000)
Cash flows T1-T5 (600 × 3.605)	2,163
Making good costs T5 (200 × 0.567)	(113.4)
NPV	49.6

A 20% increase in making good costs will require a present value of (200 × 20% × 0.567) = 22.7

The sensitivity of the 20% increase in making good costs can be estimated as 49.6 ÷ 22.7 = 218.5%

If you selected 124.0% you divided by the full increase in costs without applying the discount factor.

If you selected 1,217.6% you treated the making good costs as a cash inflow, not a cash outflow.

If you selected 45.8% you switched the numerator and denominator in your calculation.

1.9 The correct answer is: Buyer power

With 95% of its revenue derived from one customer, Company S is exposed to pressure to reduce its prices if Company O chose to demand this, or if it threatened to put its business out to tender.

1.10 The correct answer is: Assess the significance of each risk

Once risks have been identified, the next step in the risk management process is to assess each one in terms of its potential severity and its probability. Once this is done, a suitable plan for their control or mitigation can be devised, based upon where resources can be most effectively used, as some risks will be of far less significance than others.

1.11 The correct answers are:

- The risk that a new type of irrigation system will fail to find a large enough market
- The risk of competitors moving their production to a different country and being able to cut costs
- The risk of resource depletion, meaning that new sources of sheet metal will have to be found

The risk of the human resources director moving to a competitor is an example of operating risk because HR is not a primary function of the business.

1.12 The correct answers are:

- Credit risk
- Interest rate risk
- Currency risk

The biggest risk facing the bank would seem to be the risk of falling commercial property prices. This risk links to:

Credit risk: If property prices collapse, the bank will almost certainly suffer losses from defaults by borrowers.

Interest rate risk: If interest rates rise, the bank's funding costs will rise but interest income from lending may be largely fixed.

Currency risk: Most commercial property loans are in US dollars. There is a risk that a fall in the value of the US dollar would result in losses due to a fall in the value of the bank's US dollar assets and interest income.

1.13 The correct answers are:

- Increasing sensitivity of consumers to food allergies
- Consumer resistance to testing their products using animals

Allergic reactions and animal testing are significant issues for consumers which make them strategic. Food labelling is an operational risk as it relates to printing not strategy and can easily be addressed. Power cuts are also an operational risk as they are unlikely to be significant in a developed country. Individually, factory workers are unlikely to be of strategic importance; however, should the workforce choose to boycott the company en masse, that may require more of a strategic solution.

1.14 The correct answer is: Cultural risk

Cultural risk applies to an international business attempting to sell a product in another country. The other risks can apply to both domestic and international businesses.

1.15 The correct answer is: A sales initiative offering a prompt payment discount

Revenue has increased, cash is being collected quicker and receivables days have reduced from 73 days to 63 days ([20 ÷ 100] × 365 days = 73 days; [30 ÷ 175] × 365 days = 63 days). Credit control staff are not taking time to settle in as cash is being collected quicker than last year. Demand has not fallen as revenue has increased significantly. It seems credit terms are more likely to have decreased rather than increased in this case.

1.16 The correct answer is: Adverse labour cost variances

Adverse labour cost variances are most likely, as staff will work the same hours but the cost to the company will be greater. Workers will have better pay and conditions and are less likely to leave, plus in relative terms workers will be no better off switching jobs than they would have been before the change in legislation, so increased staff turnover is unlikely. Material costs may have risen to cover suppliers' own labour costs increasing, but material usage will probably not be affected by this. Labour costs will rise, meaning contract profits will fall.

1.17 The correct answer is: Loss of all data from a malicious computer virus

Pure risks are those where no benefit is derived, so no benefit can come from losing all data to malware. A stock market fall can benefit short sellers and those looking to invest. Losing a patent can actually be a good thing as it may stimulate innovation - some patents are only awarded for a fixed time anyway (such as in the pharmaceutical industry). The restriction of funds from an entity's bank may encourage more creative use of funds.

1.18 The correct answer is:

High likelihood, low impact Staff are unable to come into work due to sickness	**High likelihood, high impact** Staff create content that breaks copyright laws and the company is sued for damages
Low likelihood, low impact Staff are unable to access the office because the lift malfunctions	**Low likelihood, high impact** Staff cannot access their work because of a fire in the server room

A malfunctioning lift is unlikely to occur in a new office in a developing country - staff can still use the stairs! Sickness on an individual basis is likely but not significant (an epidemic may move this to become a higher impact issue though). Breaking copyright law is now a distinct risk as the law is not well understood and there is so much available content online that is not formally cited.

1.19 The correct answers are:

- Increased demand for its drinks
- Increased prices of its drinks

Hot weather usually makes people thirsty, so reduced supply often leads to people wishing to stockpile, which increases demand. As demand increases and supply falls, market price is likely to rise. Although demand may increase, if Company C is unable to manufacture due to supply shortages, it will not be able to sell any more drinks overall. Company C would also be unable to manufacture more drinks due to the shortage of carbon dioxide. Finally, consumers want to drink because of the hot weather, but supply is fixed, so rivals will only be able to compete on price. However, as this is a temporary problem, they may wish to keep prices stable and not reduce them so their margins are not affected.

2 Managing Risk

2.1 The correct answers are:

- Shareholders
- Lenders

Organisations are required to report their risks to shareholders and other capital providers, which would include lenders and any other capital providers. Modern day auditors' reports now include an assessment of the organisation's key risks which is primarily targeted at current and prospective investors. However, although customers, suppliers and employees have a stake in an organisation, management does not need to report risks to them as stakeholders. Government is also an interested stakeholder, but is more interested in taxation revenue and general business continuity than knowing about the risks themselves.

2.2 The correct answer is: Severity high, frequency low

Insurance might be the most appropriate risk hedging strategy when the potential cost is high, but the likelihood of the adverse outcome happening is fairly low. When the frequency is high, internal measures to manage the risk would probably be more appropriate.

2.3 The correct answer is: Avoiding investments where the risk is high if an investment offering the same return for less risk is available.

Risk aversion is not the same as risk avoidance. Risk aversion means not undertaking an investment when an alternative is available offering the same return for less risk, or a higher return for the same risk.

2.4 The correct answer is: Avoid the risk by ceasing production while the cause of the defects is identified.

This is dangerous as the reputation risk from one product could adversely affect sales of others.

2.5 The correct answer is:

Receivables days [Transfer ▼]

Gearing ratio [Reduce ▼]

Receivables days are rising suggesting that the company is unable to collect its debts on time, which may lead to liquidity issues and could be contributing to increased interest-bearing debt (eg overdraft). As interest cover is an output factor, it should be accepted, as improving cash flow should reduce short-term interest charges. Both receivables days and gearing need to be reduced, but as each response needs to be different, the risk associated with debt collection could be transferred to a third-party factoring agency, allowing the company to reduce its debt levels (this is an active choice as an increase in liquid cash could be paid out to shareholders, but the desire to manage debt levels is favoured here).

2.6 The correct answer is: Access restrictions on assets

Access restrictions are control procedures, which are normally distinguished from the control environment.

2.7 The correct answer is:

A customer or third party may be killed or injured by an accident caused by a manufacturing flaw.

[Transfer ▼]

Environmental legislation in Germany is likely to require cars sold there to comply with stringent emissions and fuel economy standards that are impossible for cars of this type.

Avoid ▼

The damages caused by such an event are best addressed by transferring this risk via insurance. Such risks could not be accepted or avoided, and while reduction may reduce the likelihood, the impact remains the same.

It appears impossible to comply with this legislation, so it cannot be accepted, reduced or transferred, meaning that avoidance (such as not selling in Germany) is the only option.

2.8 The correct answer is: Risk hedging is taking action to offset one risk by incurring a new risk in the opposite direction.

Some operational risks will be high frequency, high severity risks. The management of a portfolio of different risks is risk pooling or risk diversification. Insurance companies will insist that businesses take some action to reduce many risks as a condition of insuring those risks.

2.9 The correct answers are:

- Risk seeking
- Risk aversion

Risk aversion and risk seeking are two extremes of an organisation's risk appetite – risk-averse organisations do not seek higher risk investments unless compensated by higher returns, while risk seekers focus on maximising their returns, regardless of the risk.

Risk tolerance refers to the range of risks that the organisation can tolerate, while risk capacity describes the assets that the organisation uses to take risks and absorb losses. Crucially though, these do not take into account the views of investors who ultimately decide on an acceptable balance between risk and reward.

2.10 The correct answer is: Transfer

You could have reached this conclusion from a common-sense perspective by identifying that the warning label is a disclaimer similar to those seen on many common items (eg 'Warning – contents may be hot' on a takeaway coffee cup) which protects the company from any legal action that may be brought against it by a customer who suffers damage from consuming their product. The warning is seen as a way of legally transferring risk onto the consumer (similar to a 'buyer beware' scenario in many transactions).

This could also have the TARA model applied to it – the likelihood of an allergic reaction occurring in anyone eating a snack produced by a 'reputable' manufacturer (probably in a highly regulated industry) is low, but could be potentially serious (even life-threatening in extreme cases) so risk transfer appears the most likely option here.

2.11 The correct answers are:

- Information, communication and reporting
- Governance and culture
- Strategy and objective setting
- Performance
- Review and revision

These are all five of the COSO internal control components.

2.12 The correct answer is: Management of the risk associated with stakeholder conflicts

The COSO enterprise risk management framework helps the organisation to apply the TARA risk management model. It also allows the organisation to allocate capital on a considered basis, and also helps to ensure that risk management becomes part of the culture of the organisation, embedded into all its processes and activities. However, the COSO framework gives no guidance on the influence of stakeholders, even though their objectives may conflict with those of the organisation.

2.13 The correct answers are:

- Outsource its IT function
- Make sure that contingency plans and procedures are in place and well understood

For a risk that is of high severity but low frequency, it is necessary to make contingency plans in case the breakdown occurs. Outsourcing the IT function is also a possibility for transferring the risk, as long as there is a service level agreement (SLA) in place which protects the hospital in the event of system breakdowns. Closing the affected department is an example of avoiding/abandoning the risk, which is a suitable response to risks that are regarded as high severity and high frequency. Keeping the situation under review (acceptance) is a suitable response to a risk that is regarded as low severity and low frequency.

2.14 The correct answer is: Transfer

An insurance policy may be used to transfer a risk to another party (the insurer). Not all risks are insurable, for example the risk that a product will become obsolete or out-of-date due to advances in technology.

Risk reduction involves taking action to control or reduce risk.

Risk acceptance involves not taking any action.

Risk avoidance would require abandoning the project.

2.15 The correct answers are:

- Paying unskilled employees a 'living wage' in excess of the minimum wage
- Sponsoring a local children's sports team

Paying a 'living wage' in excess of the minimum wage would cost the organisation money and would be perceived as 'doing the right thing'. Sponsoring a local children's football team would also be perceived as socially responsible.

Encouraging a 'work-hard play-hard' culture is likely to be perceived as irresponsible.

Relocating a customer service call centre to an area with high unemployment is likely to be perceived as a commercial decision (for example to take advantage of a relatively cheap source of labour) rather than as a decision taken in the wider interest of society.

Reducing the risk of a component failing by importing the component would lead to increased pollution and carbon footprint from the transportation required.

2.16 The correct answer is: Identify the key facts and ethical issues and consider alternative courses of action.

Use the following approach to ethical dilemmas:

1 Identify the key facts (briefly).
2 Identify the relevant ethical issues and fundamental principles.
3 Consider alternatives and their consequences.
4 Make a recommendation and justify it.

2.17 The correct answers are:

- Proportionate to the level of risk faced
- Comprehensive
- Dynamic and responsive to emerging risks
- Influence of human and cultural factors

Communication and consultation is listed as part of the risk management process within ISO 31000, while allocation of roles and responsibilities is listed as part of the risk management framework within ISO 31000.

ANSWERS

2.18 The correct answers are:

- Promoting enterprise risk management across the company
- Developing risk management policies
- Designing risk indicators

Reviewing existing systems of internal control for risks are most likely to be undertaken by either internal or external auditor (although the risk manager will be interested in the output from such reviews) while determining the company's risk appetite would be the responsibility of either the board or a risk committee.

2.19 The correct answer is: Senior management own and operate the first two lines, while the third line reports directly to the board.

Senior management operates the first line of defence, the board operates the second and the third is usually carried out by the external auditors - this is incorrect because the board is only involved in the third line of defence and the third is carried out by the internal, not external auditors.

There is no separation between the first two lines of defence, but the third is managed by a separate part of the organisation – this is almost correct, but the first and second lines are separate because the first line owns the risk and the controls necessary to manage that risk, while the second line is a management or oversight function that is separate from the first line.

The three lines of defence model is not used by external auditors (although they can add to the assurance already present in the organisation).

2.20 The correct answer is: Responses to address each risk.

Responses to address each risk are the most likely addition to C's risk register. Timescales are possible but not as likely as responses. Sponsors are too high level to put in the risk register while insurance is also incorrect as not every risk will be addressed by insurance.

3 Strategy, Reputation and Risk

3.1 The correct answers are:

- Operational
- Legal
- Reputation

F has implemented controls and procedures aimed at reducing the chance of a similar incident happening again, thus reducing its operational risk and the risk of further legal action from affected employees in the future. By publicising the action that was taken, the company should also be able to improve its reputation, which is likely to have been damaged in the local community.

Financial risk is not relevant in this scenario as it refers to issues related to cash flows, economic factors and fraud.

3.2 The correct answer is: Complete a review of the marketplace

The other options will not address changes to the digital landscape (eg streaming to portable devices).

3.3 The correct answer is: How the organisation creates value over time

The primary purpose of an integrated report is to explain how the organisation creates value over time. Integrated reporting differs from other forms of reporting in that it focuses on the process not the product, using a series of capitals to illustrate how an organisation creates value for all stakeholders. The report is concerned with the organisation's ability to continue to draw on these capitals over time.

3.4 The correct answers are:

- The value creation process
- Value creation over time
- The capitals

The three fundamental concepts underpinning are:

The 'capitals' are the resources and the relationships used and affected by the organisation. They are: financial, manufactured, human, intellectual, natural and social. An organisation's integrated report is not required to cover all capitals, it should focus on the capitals relevant to the entity.

The 'value creation process' is in effect an entity's business model. This explains how capitals and inputs are transformed by the entity's activities to create outputs and outcomes.

'Value creation over time' relates to the organisation's ability to continue to draw on these capitals in a continuous cycle.

3.5 The correct answers are:

- A change in national government
- An increase in digital technology

A change in national government may change policy on educational standards or funding, which will be of strategic importance to N. An increase in digital technology is also relevant to N as this will require greater investment in such technology to attract students. Any economic uncertainty may affect the affordability of education, which could affect demand for N's courses.

Changes in local infrastructure, such as roads and telecommunications, are not relevant as students will probably enroll regardless. A decline in the birth rate is also not relevant as it is not just young people who go to university! A change in local government will also have no real direct influence on education either.

3.6 The correct answer is: We want to put the news in your hand wherever you are

The other mission statements ignore the declining print market, but this recognises innovation and the impact of digital disruption.

None of the other mission statements focus on market share or the declining print market.

3.7 The correct answer is: Reducing spending on research and development

Reducing spending on research and development would be risky for G because it is unlikely to maintain its position if no new products are developed.

Outsourcing its payroll function to save costs would have limited risk impact, while implementing home-working for app developers would actually lead to lower establishment costs and overheads, as would relocating to smaller premises.

3.8 The correct answer is: A new entrant who provides similar products at a lower price

A new entrant who provides similar products at a lower price would lead to M's differentiation losing value, meaning that this could be a serious competitor.

The emergence of a low-cost competitor would not be significant for M as it is not competing as a cost leader.

New technology might be available across the market but the impact would be shared across the market and is unlikely to act as a disruption to domestic appliances like dishwashers and washing machines in the same way as digital technology has disrupted other markets.

An underlying increase in raw material and component prices would affects all players in the market but cost leaders will feel the impact on their margins the most.

3.9 The correct answer is: Increase its advertising spend and run a series of promotions for its existing products

Increasing advertising spend and running a series of promotions for existing products is penetration, which maintains N's position at minimal levels of risk.

Developing a range of footwear for use in the construction industry is diversification, which for a new product in a new market is very risky due to guaranteed investment expenditure but no guarantee of success (N's shareholders are risk averse).

Exporting its current products to neighbouring countries is market development, which would also be risky as products may not sell there.

Offering high-quality knitwear products to its existing customers represents product development: this is also risky as there is no guarantee that customers will like this and it may affect demand for existing products.

3.10 The correct answers are:

- Customers
- Information team

Taking each stakeholder in turn, using the Mendelow grid to assess them:

- Employees: low power, low interest (or are just not bothered) which leads to minimal effort
- Customers: high power and also high interest, so they become key players
- Paper suppliers: high interest, low power, so they should be kept informed
- Shareholders: high power, low interest, so keep them satisfied
- Information team: high power over the implementation and high interest in its success which also makes them key players

3.11 The correct answer is: Maintain current spend but innovate via research and development

Maintaining current spend but innovating via research and development is appropriate for P because the product has reached maturity and is unable to continue for much longer in its current form.

Increasing production would relate to a product that was still growing.

Spending more on marketing: although this might help X stand out against new entrants, that would apply better to a product with some life left, currently at the shakeout phase of the product life cycle.

Withdrawing the product immediately would only potentially apply if the product was in decline.

3.12 The correct answer is: Reduced sales

Not all customers want to pay with cards, so sales will be affected (at least in the short to medium term). This is also unlikely to affect the overall shopping experience as prices and products are not affected. Without any cash on site, armed robberies will disappear, while transactions will not require cash to be changed.

3.13 The correct answers are:

- New legislation
- Availability of labour and materials
- Export limits on sales

New legislation is likely due to the departure from the existing legal framework. The availability of labour and materials will also be affected as these may be in short supply if the region cannot interact as easily with its neighbours. Export limits on sales are also a risk as it may be possible that deals in other countries are less straightforward than those currently in place.

Currency risk is not relevant, as B currently exports anyway, so this exposure already exists. New governance requirements for B and capital availability are not mentioned, so are not relevant to B (although in other similar scenarios capital may not flow as easily across borders as before).

3.14 The correct answer is: Errors in estimating the likely production capacity required

Errors in estimating the likely production capacity required are most likely to be mitigated by this activity, because knowing what you are likely to sell allows you to model production demands accordingly.

We are told that the product is ready to launch, so research and development expenditure is unlikely to be affected. Marketing is unlikely to be driven by sales volumes, so the budget is unlikely to be affected by this activity.

The scenario planning aims to understand volumes not specifications, so copyright infringement is not relevant here (legal action is also unlikely because the market research would have helped to identify similar products, so the company is less likely to launch a copy).

3.15 The correct answer is: The organisation's strategy should consider the actions of its competitors as well as its own actions.

The organisation should consider a range of possible outcomes from current trends as part of its strategic analysis - this is foresight (consideration of different outcomes is possible in game theory, but the analysis of trends is more likely to apply to foresight).

A panel of experts is used to speculate about future developments and consider possible responses - this is a think tank.

Experts are approached in isolation and asked for their opinions on strategic questions - this is the Delphi method.

3.16 The correct answer is: Profitability assessment

Profitability assessment is included in the UK Bank of England stress testing methodology.

Minimum capital amounts, visibility of risks and improved disclosures are all included in Basel III.

3.17 The correct answers are:

- Legal action from US and UK authorities
- Legal action from the authorities in its own country
- Adverse impact on share price
- Reputation risk

All options are likely risks that the company will face due to legislation and other reputational impacts.

3.18 The correct answer is: The risk that you are perceived differently as a result of the adverse consequences of another risk

The risk of untruthful or misleading behaviour by one or more participants in a particular process is probity risk.

The risk of not adhering to a set of moral principles is ethical risk.

The risks from offering an inducement for someone to perform their actions improperly is bribery risk.

3.19 The correct answer is: Improve the cleanliness of engines so they meet the minimum cleanliness standards

Improving the cleanliness of engines so they meet the minimum cleanliness standards is the most important thing that V needs to do first, as the emissions are a legal requirement.

Continuing to manufacture vehicles and engines in the same way as before would not address their 'dirty' engines, so needs to be addressed as a priority.

While communicating their apologies to all stakeholders and changing the governance structure of the company to avoid similar scandals in future are positive steps (and quite logical), they don't help V to address the issue of their 'dirty' engines.

3.20 The correct answer is: A is only interested in making money, regardless of the impact on its workforce

The perception is that A's strategy places money above everything else. This is what a reputation is. Saying 'A is a low-cost online retailer that offers a wide range of products and great customer service' feels more like a brand statement that differentiates it from its competitors rather than the perception of others. Saying that 'A is a terrible company to work for' feels like it is only written from the viewpoint of its employees. 'A should be more like its competitors who value their staff' says more about other companies' reputations than it does about A's.

4 Governance Risk

4.1 The correct answers are:

- The recruitment of NEDs with experience outside the industry the organisation operates in
- Full disclosure of director remuneration
- A clear distinction between the roles of chair and chief executive officer

4.2 The correct answer is: To consider and safeguard the interests of shareholders

This is part of Agency Theory.

4.3 The correct answers are:

Audit	**The Committee responsible for liaising with external audit, supervising internal audit and reviewing the annual accounts and internal controls**
Remuneration	**The Committee responsible for advising on executive director salary and other rewards for directors**
Risk	**The Committee responsible for overseeing how prepared the organisation is to respond to possible threats**
Nominations	**The Committee responsible for recommending the appointments of new directors to the board**

4.4 The correct answer is: The reliance of shareholders on directors to run the company

Agency Theory assumes that agent and principal act in their own self-interest. The separation of ownership from management results in shareholders relying upon agents (directors) to run the company for them.

4.5 The correct answers are:

- A Nominations Committee that oversees the appointment of new directors
- A wide range of backgrounds and experience across board members
- A well-respected, strong CEO

An effective Nominations Committee is an important element of a board of directors, ensuring appropriate procedures are followed for board member appointment and rotation. A diverse board ensures a wider range of views are considered. A strong CEO is generally a positive, as effective leadership requires a strong, decisive mind. If this option had included the word 'dominant' or the phrase 'unwilling to listen' it would then be correct to exclude this when identifying desirable factors.

Linking 80% of director remuneration to the achievement of current year financial targets would encourage the board to favour actions that produce short-term results over investments that may be more beneficial overall, but would deliver results later.

4.6 The correct answers are:

The view of an individual non-executive director should always carry more weight than the view of an individual executive director.	False
The view of an individual executive director should always carry more weight than the view of an individual non-executive director.	False
When considering the make-up and balance of the board, the number and status of non-executive directors should be sufficient to ensure their views carry significant weight.	True

The views of individual directors should always be judged on their merits. When considering the 'inside out mix' of executive directors and NEDs. It is important that the number and status of non-executive directors is sufficient to ensure their views carry significant weight.

4.7 The correct answer is: Review of succession planning within the organisation

Succession planning is a matter of strategy that the board as a whole would normally consider.

4.8 The correct answer is: The nomination committee should consist entirely of executive directors.

Corporate governance practice varies, but the UK Corporate Governance Code recommends that the majority of nomination committee members should be independent NEDs.

4.9 The correct answer is: They should have no shareholdings in the company

While owning shares can present a conflict of interest, most governance codes (eg UK Corporate Governance Code) specify that independence can be compromised only if such shareholdings are significant. The remaining answers (pensions, length of service and previous employment) are far more likely to compromise independence.

4.10 The correct answer is: The board act as an agent of shareholders and have access to more information than shareholders.

The board act on behalf of shareholders. Shareholders have relatively restricted access to information, for example shareholders do not usually have the right to inspect the detailed financial records of the organisation. Shareholders usually base their judgement of future prospects on the annual report and accounts, stockbrokers' reports and media sources. This situation, where the agent has more information that the principal, is referred to as an 'information asymmetry'.

4.11 The correct answers are:

- More bureaucratic
- Less accountability

Disadvantages of multi-tier boards include that they are more bureaucratic and can lead to confusion over authority and accountability.

Advantages of multi-tier boards include greater independence from operational pressures and broader representation from the inclusion of a wider range of stakeholders.

4.12 The correct answer is: A charity will have different reporting responsibilities and committee structure.

A charity will have different reporting responsibilities (for example, for charities based in England and Wales, to the Charity Commission) and committee structure. Strategy, internal controls and financial objectives are important to charities. Charites set goals and are responsible for the funds they receive and spend.

4.13 The correct answers are:

- A focus on short-term profitability rather than long-term profitability
- Domination of the board by a single individual

4.14 The correct answers are:

- Lack of true independence
- Lack of a wider perspective

4.15 The correct answer is: Enables the board to better understand the environment and market

Ensuring diversity across an organisation, including at board level, enables the organisation to more readily understand the environment and market.

The other options imply diversity is something that is done for the sake of appearance or to appease others. This should not be the case - diversity should make commercial sense.

4.16 The correct answer is: Being responsible for developing new investment initiatives

This would normally be the responsibility of the chief executive officer.

4.17 The correct answers are:

- The company can satisfactorily appoint an audit committee from its existing employees
- The company can satisfactorily recommend the appointment of further directors using its existing employees
- The company can satisfactorily oversee the internal audit function using its existing employees.

Audit committees require at least three NEDs unless the company is small, when only two are required. Company J has only just become big enough to need to adopt corporate governance best practice so the two NEDs currently employed are sufficient. However, while they have enough NEDs, they are not suitably qualified for the demands of the audit committee due to not having any financial experience. This will also mean that they are unlikely to be able to appoint external auditors.

However, the existing NEDs understand the business well enough to currently manage the internal audit team so could continue to fulfil this role.

The appointment of further directors is usually undertaken by the board but recommendations usually come from the nominations committee which only needs the majority of it to be NEDs to follow corporate governance best practice, so could be undertaken using existing employees.

4.18 The correct answer is: Basic pay and share options that vest in three years' time

Basic pay and share options that vest in three years' time represents an appropriate mixture of fixed and variable elements with a long-term viewpoint to promote value creation.

Basic pay fixed for each day worked by the director in any given month sounds variable and feels more like a non-executive director's remuneration (plus there is no incentive to perform).

Basic pay and a bonus based on the current year's performance by the company sounds plausible but only basing it on one year feels quite short term.

Basic pay, pension, healthcare benefits and a company car - this package is not all basic pay, but there is no performance element included either, so is also inappropriate.

4.19 The correct answer is: The company has decided to focus on short-term growth to satisfy its directors.

The company has decided to focus on short-term growth to satisfy its directors: although shareholders will see some benefit in the short term, directors are the ones most likely to benefit from this change, because while they are being paid directly from profits, the company's strategy is likely to erode the company's value over time, making shareholders poorer in the long term.

The company has adopted a new risk appetite to become more of a risk seeker than in previous years: this may be true but is not conclusive from the scenario.

The company has added value to its brand by improving its offering to customers: actually, the opposite is true as there is now less investment in research and development to improve products.

The company has decided to focus on long-term growth to satisfy its shareholders: clearly, shareholders will be happy with the imminent rise in dividend, but without investment in research and development the company is unlikely to grow in such a competitive environment

4.20 The correct answer is: Strategy will be accepted on the basis of financial factors alone

Strategy will be accepted on the basis of financial factors alone because without NEDs, there will be no-one to challenge the decisions of the board.

The company will not pursue a strategy of significant growth and expansion because with board members mostly paid a fixed sum and a clear desire to limit costs, there is no evidence to support this.

The company will probably not undertake research and development into alternative foods that may not sell because that would probably be perceived as unnecessary expenditure in a stable market.

Directors will not decide to pursue a risk-seeking strategy that could affect profits because the absence of performance-related pay does not support this approach to risk either.

5 Internal Control Systems

5.1 The correct answer is:

Deterioration in relationships with customers and suppliers	**Dealings with customers and suppliers are on the terms that have been agreed**
Failure to receive income that is due to the organisation	**Establishment of a credit control department**
Deterioration in the value of assets	**Physical safeguards against theft or damage**
Transactions being completed without adequate authorisation	**Maintenance of a list of approved signatories**

5.2 The correct answers are:

- Store security staff to check employees' bags at random when they are leaving the shop
- All goods should carry electronic tags that trigger alarms at store exits unless the goods have been scanned through the EPOS terminals/tills
- Monthly independent inventory counts to be undertaken by staff from other shops or from head office, with the results compared to inventory records

Random employee bag checks would discourage staff from stealing inventory.

Ensuring goods are purchased by the head office buying department, and that prices are set by head office would not reduce the opportunity for inventory fraud.

Having all goods carry electronic tags that trigger alarms at store exits unless scanned would both discourage and detect theft.

Independent inventory counts would reduce the chance of collusion.

5.3 The correct answer is: Comparison of goods received notes with purchase orders

This comparison is a check that goods and services received have been authorised.

5.4 The correct answer is: Comparison of bank paying-in slips with initial receipt records

Daily bankings will help reduce the risk of monies received not being banked but do not ensure that monies don't go astray during the day. Listing the amounts received and issuing receipts are important recording controls, but the most important check is a comparison of what has actually been banked with what has been received.

5.5 The correct answer is: Hedging policy statement

Hedging is designed to combat excessive risks. Whilst the organisation may face a serious shortage of cash if it takes excessive risks, a hedging policy will not have any impact on temporary cash trading shortages or funds being tied in long-term investment.

5.6 The correct answer is: A tangible non-current assets register containing cost and accumulated depreciation of each asset

Where a tangible non-current asset register is maintained, that contains cost and progressively records accumulated depreciation in respect of each asset, this should ensure that further depreciation cannot be charged once the asset has been fully written off, provided that the annual depreciation is calculated from this information.

5.7 The correct answer is: ROCE

Each store is an investment centre, therefore the measure used needs to take into account the capital invested in each store. Return on capital employed (ROCE) is the only measure of the four suggested that does this. However, J would have to be careful that the use of ROCE did not encourage 'short-termism', particularly a reluctance to invest in the stores.

5.8 The correct answers are:

- A control system will assist in compliance with laws and regulations.
- The introduction of a control system is overdue.
- The introduction of a control system will change the way the business operates.

A control system will help ensure financial results are timely and accurate, taxation compliance and other regulatory compliance.

The point of a control system is to manage risks that may hinder the fulfilment of objectives. Just because the objectives are being fulfilled, does not mean that potential risks should be ignored.

The introduction of a control system is overdue because the business has grown and employs a large number of staff.

The fact that the employees are creative individuals will not mean that a control system is unnecessary. Creative people may be able to think of ways of defrauding the business!

The introduction of a control system will change the way the business operates, for example through more formal processes and checks.

5.9 The correct answers are:

- Grow branch revenue
- Control branch costs

Profit centre managers are responsible for revenues and costs. They have no investment responsibilities. Expanding the branch network would require investment.

5.10 The correct answers are:
Ensuring time sheets are signed by supervisors would act as an authorisation control and would reduce the chance of staff claiming for more hours than they worked.

Confirming information with suppliers (for example by checking the amount showing as owing on J Co's system matches the amount showing as due from J Co on the supplier's system) would help prevent overpayment. The separate buying department control is more applicable to the prevention of goods being ordered for personal use.

Theft of portable equipment would be discouraged by CCTV coverage. However, the benefits must outweigh the cost. Detailed asset registers are unlikely to prevent theft although they would help to detect theft after the event.

5.11 The correct answers are:

- The business does not pay too much for goods and services.
- The business researches potential suppliers before contracting with them.

Both of these objectives are answered by the control of putting contracts out to tender.

'The business has a central database of suppliers' is not a control objective, it is a control, to ensure that goods and services are purchased from approved suppliers. 'The business has goods and services when it needs them' is a control objective, but it is not directly answered by the control set out in the question. A tender process does not ensure that receipt of goods will be timely. Similarly, 'the business does not purchase goods and services from connected parties' is a control objective, but it is not answered by the control of receiving tenders. A tendering process might help prevent a company dealing with related parties while being unaware that they are connected, but does not completely prevent it. For example, if the connected party is a large concern, there might be nothing or no one attached to the tender that would appear to be connected to the purchasing company.

5.12 The correct answer is: Review of accounting records to see if expenditure on non-current assets has been included as capital expenditure

How assets are treated in the financial accounts should not impact upon how the organisation takes steps to ensure their safe custody.

5.13 The correct answer is: Statement 2 is true and Statement 1 is false.

It is not possible to eliminate risk (without ceasing operations). In commercial organisations, profit is part of the reward for successful risk taking. The purpose of an internal control system is to manage and control risk rather than to eliminate it. So Statement 1 is false.

Statement 2 is true. COSO states 'Internal control is a process affected by an entity's board of directors, management and other personnel, designed to provide reasonable assurance regarding the achievement of objectives'.

5.14 The correct answers are:

- Safeguard the shareholders' investment
- Manage and control business risk

Reduced time needed for an external audit and maximising profitability may be by-products of an effective internal control system, but they are not the main benefits of an effective system.

5.15 The correct answer is:

Statement 1 is true because by counting the inventory P is checking that the number of parts which T has issued is consistent with the number of parts that should have been issued according to the parts requisitions.

Statement 2 is false. If a fraudulent parts requisition was issued the parts in stock could still match the requisitions, in which case P would be unaware of the fraud.

5.16 The correct answers are:

- Customer satisfaction measures
- Group target measures rather than individual measures
- Differentiate between simple and complex queries and measure these separately

Introducing a target call resolution time would likely adversely impact the quality of service provided and make staff reluctant to take on more complex calls. The same problem, the prioritisation of speed over the quality of service, would also apply if a target minimum number of calls was introduced.

The scorecard should be used to monitor group and organisational performance, rather than the performance of specific individuals.

5.17 The correct answer is: The analysis of those items where performance differs significantly from standard or budget

5.18 The correct answer is: Strategic plan

Standard costing and Activity-based management are both quantitative approaches to control while the balanced scorecard uses a mixture of financial and non-financial controls.

5.19 The correct answer is:

Unless the alloy wheel business unit is obligated to supply BMC they are likely to prioritise external sales.	**True**
Unless appropriate adjustments are made, the planned approach will distort the financial performance of the alloy wheel business unit.	**True**
It is not possible to set realistic financial performance targets to the alloy wheel business unit under these circumstances.	**False**

5.20 The correct answer is: Whether the advice provided enabled customers to better manage their finances.

The customer perspective is concerned with the quality of the service provided. For a budgetary advisory service, the main indicator of service quality is whether the advice provided enabled customers to better manage their finances.

The other options would be classified as internal business (processes) or innovation and learning (staff turnover, number of qualified staff) in the balanced scorecard.

5.21 The correct answers are:

- A motor vehicle manufacturer
- A mobile phone manufacturer
- A commercial printing company

Economic value added (EVA) is based on the premise that businesses should create returns at a rate above their cost of capital. The EVA calculation depends heavily on invested capital due to the way the capital charge is calculated. It is most suited to companies with relatively high levels or values of assets. The three organisations selected would all have significant investment in tangible physical assets including plant and machinery.

5.22 The correct answer is: Capture organisational learning and document it to ensure lessons are learnt

CIMA define a post-completion audit as 'an objective, independent assessment of the success of a project in relation to plan. It covers the whole life of the project and provides feedback to managers to aid the implementation and control of future projects.'

The audit is not intended as a means of directly appraising the performance of the project manager, or of obtaining sign-off on project documentation, or of closing budgetary codes.

5.23 The correct answer is: Describe a specific, required project outcome

Project objectives need to be SMART (Specific, Measurable, Achievable, Relevant, Time-bound). Objectives that meet this criteria are then able to be used in project monitoring and control.

The other options refer to some useful information that should be considered and documented, but they relate to issues that are wider than individual project objectives.

5.24 The correct answer is: Ensuring the fitness for purpose of deliverables

Quality is concerned with fitness for purpose. In a project management content the focus should ultimately be on ensuring the project deliverables are produced to specification - which means to the required level of quality.

The aim should be to ensure quality during the project, rather than a reliance on the inspection and testing of output.

Lessons relevant to quality may be learned during the post-completion audit, but the main focus should be on ensuring the fitness for purpose of project deliverables.

In this context, the presentation of project reports is a relatively minor issue.

5.25 The correct answers are:

- Improved decision making
- Better researched projects
- Improved internal controls
- Highlight reasons for successful projects

CIMA define a post-completion audit as 'an objective, independent assessment of the success of a project in relation to plan. It covers the whole life of the project and provides feedback to managers to aid the implementation and control of future projects.'

Over time, by highlighting things that worked well and things that didn't, these audits will facilitate improved decision making, improved internal controls and better researched projects.

The process is not necessarily quick and inexpensive. The time and cost will depend to a large extent on the complexity of the project.

5.26 The correct answers are:

- Staff are trained on new equipment
- Daily production logs and failure rates are noted

A good or effective control environment, that would either help identify the causes of waste or reduce the likelihood for waste, would include staff receiving adequate training on new equipment and records being kept that recorded production levels and failures.

Judging the performance of production line managers based on the volume of production would encourage managers to push lines to the limit, sacrificing quality for quantity.

Involving senior management in operational inspections is not practical. Line inspections and the checking of calibrations should be performed daily or more, at least until the level of wastage is reduced.

5.27 The correct answer is: Post-completion audit report

A cost-benefit review cannot be carried out until after the project has been completed and implemented operationally. This is a task for the post-completion audit. The purpose of a completion report is to document the completion of the project, with the client or project user signing off.

5.28 The correct answers are:

- Post-completion audits could produce valuable insights
- Post-completion audits will not prevent dysfunctional behaviour by project sponsors
- It may be difficult to introduce post-completion audits

CIMA define a post-completion audit as 'an objective, independent assessment of the success of a project in relation to plan. It covers the whole life of the project and provides feedback to managers to aid the implementation and control of future projects.'

It would not be reasonable or appropriate to find the project sponsor liable for all negative findings from post-completion audits. Project shortcomings should be investigated and those responsible held accountable, although in many situations a combination of factors and stakeholders contribute to the failing.

Judging the performance of production line managers based on the volume of production would encourage managers to push lines to the limit, sacrificing quality for quantity.

A post-completion audit can be completed retrospectively. This would be worthwhile for some past projects at Z, to enable lessons to be learned.

5.29 The correct answers are:

- To ensure the system is secure
- To ensure the system meets the needs of managers
- To ensure the system produces accurate information

A post-implementation review establishes whether the objectives and targeted performance criteria for the new system have been met.

Examples of relevant measures include:

- Ensuring the system is secure
- Ensuring the system meets the needs of users
- Ensuring the system produces accurate information
- Measuring throughput speeds on new systems and comparing them with prior performance
- The volume and nature of errors and queries (both quantitative and qualitative)
- Comparison of the new system costs compared with the amount budgeted

Although a comparison of cost versus budget may form part of the post-implementation review, the review would not establish the costs incurred on the project, as this would have already been done. The time taken on the project would also be established before the post-implementation review.

5.30 The correct answer is: Raising concerns when asked to perform a specialised task outside your expertise

The fundamental principle of professional competence and due care requires an individual to only undertake tasks that they are confident they have the skills to perform. This may mean undergoing training before undertaking a task, or working with a more experienced colleague to gain the skills and expertise required.

5.31 The correct answer is: Earning a $150,000 salary

The accountant will wish to continue to be paid the salary. However the salary is likely to be less dependent on the company's results, and hence offer less of a temptation to manipulate results, than the other options.

5.32 The correct answer is: Lack of a proper job description when the accountant was recruited.

This may have an impact on an assignment, but the accountant may be able to complete an assignment without it. The other options have more direct impact on an assignment.

5.33 The correct answer is:

F has threatened to sack its auditors following a disagreement over the value of inventory in the financial statements.	**Intimidation**
An audit partner has written a letter from his firm to his local paper, setting out a client's case in a lawsuit.	**Advocacy**
Financial statements prepared by the Small Business Services department of T & B, an audit firm, are due to be audited by another T & B department.	**Self-review**
An audit partner has recently bought a large number of shares in a client company.	**Self-interest**
The manager of the audit of C is the brother of C's finance director.	**Familiarity**

6 Risk Management and Internal Control

6.1 The correct answer is:

Authorisation	**All overtime worked on production is approved by the production manager.**
Information processing	**Changes to company IT applications can only be made by authorised system administrators.**
Performance review	**The finance department compares actual quarterly results against budget.**
Physical controls	**Access to the computer servers is restricted to IT department staff using a system of key cards.**
Segregation of duties	**The bank reconciliation is performed by the financial manager and all banking is done by the accounts clerk.**

6.2 The correct answer is:

A member of staff checks invoices from suppliers against goods received notes before they are paid.	**Prevent**
The credit controller chases customers who have exceeded their credit period.	**Direct**
All customer services staff are given training and a procedures manual.	**Direct**

Checking invoices against goods received notes before payment prevents incorrect payment. It is therefore a prevent control.

Direct controls are controls that direct activities or staff towards a desired outcome. Chasing customers for payment is an attempt to 'direct payment'. Providing training and information relating to procedures is 'directing staff behaviour'.

6.3 The correct answer is: Sequential numbering of blank order forms

Sequential numbering is a control over the completeness of recording of orders.

6.4 The correct answers are:

- Collusion and misappropriation of inventory
- Failure to make a permanent record of inventory

Errors in counting are unlikely due to the controls used by CT Co. Inventory should not deteriorate in the time between inspections, so any faulty products are likely to be identified before they present a risk.

6.5 The correct answer is: The main reason control is exercised over employees is to prevent fraud.

Although one reason control is exercised over employees is to prevent fraud, it is incorrect to say this is the main reason.

The main reason control is exercised over employees is to ensure that their work contributes to achievement of the organisation's goals.

Employment contracts include terms related to unacceptable conduct and notice periods - so they are one way of exercising control over employees.

HR controls are more likely to be weak in smaller organisations, as these organisations tend to be more informal. There is also a chance that the business may be dominated by a single individual who may not recognise the need for formal controls.

6.6 The correct answer is: Receivables ledger and cash receipts

Teeming and lading involves diverting cash intended for one receivable to the account of another. This requires that the individual has access to cash receipts and the receivables ledger.

The other three options do not provide access to cash receipts.

6.7 The correct answers are:

- Insufficient checks on the need for additional staff
- Insufficient checks on employee identification, qualifications and background
- Lack of staff training
- Insufficient control over the overtime approval process

Four additional staff have been employed on the strength of a request from one person. Additional authorisation should be required to ensure the need for additional staff is genuine.

People should not be employed without proper checks on their identity, background, qualifications and employment history. Without these checks, the organisation could employ individuals who hide their past or exaggerate their credentials - or who don't exist (a 'ghost employee').

Staff training is an important control. If M Co HR staff had been trained in the possible risks of not following a proper employment process, they might not have employed the four recruits without checks.

S is able to approve overtime without referring to any other manager or senior person. The control issue is with the approval process rather than a lack of segregation between approval (S) and payment (payroll staff).

6.8 The correct answers are:

- False invoices could be paid
- Inferior quality goods could be accepted

Checking invoices to orders would reduce the risk of accepting invoices for goods which were not ordered. Without this check, false invoices may be paid.

It is unlikely that goods will be stolen if they have come from a preferred supplier.

As no check is made on goods received, it is possible that inferior goods will be accepted. For example, goods may have been damaged in transit.

As materials are used straight away, there is no inventory store.

6.9 The correct answer is:

Opening 24 hours a day, 7 days a week, with H working many 12-hour shifts himself. As a consequence, customer service levels have suffered.	**Tunnel vision**
Including the first day of the following month's trading in the previous month.	**Misrepresentation**
Offering unsustainable 'bargain prices' to entice customers away from competitor shops.	**Myopia**

Tunnel vision involves focusing on performance measures to the detriment of other areas.

Misrepresentation involves creative reporting to suggest that a result is acceptable.

Myopia refers to short-sightedness. In a business context it involves prioritising short-term goals at the expense of longer-term objectives.

6.10 The correct answer is:

(a) Transfer costs may mean that profit and ROI is low and frustration will arise as they do not have a wide enough product range = R

(b) The main emphasis should be on technical efficiency and quality. ROI may conflict with these aims and the division may not replace machinery as it could worsen ROI = P

(c) This division must work closely with the other two divisions and being a profit centre may not be the best option = P

Careful reading of the scenario and of the options in this type of question often reveals the answer. For example, the only division that works with both of the other two divisions is the Production Division. The only mention of machinery is the P production line. The retail division will have to absorb the cost-plus transfer prices applied by both the F and P divisions, which will reduce profit and ROI.

Frustration will appear in R because they can only source their products from P.

6.11 The correct answers are:

- Queue lengths at tills
- Customer satisfaction scores
- Number of customer complaints

Number of returns is likely to be a performance indicator for the CSF of offering the correct quality and range of products. Employee satisfaction scores will be a performance indicator for the CSF of having a happy and motivated workforce.

6.12 The correct answers are:

- The steering committee monitors the system implementation and the specific deliverables against the project plan. It has overall responsibility to ensure the system is delivered to the required time, cost and quality.
- The steering committee brings together the sponsor of the project, the project manager who is responsible for the day-to-day delivery of the project, specialist IT staff with responsibility for delivering the project and user representatives with responsibility for accepting the system.

The role and responsibilities of the steering committee are as explained in the two correct options. These are relatively high-level, rather than hands-on, operational tasks.

Setting the detailed budget is a more operational task that would likely be performed by the project manager.

Ethical implications should be considered before a project is given the go-ahead, before a steering committee is established.

Control implications may be considered at a high level by the steering committee, but the detailed needs of internal auditors would not be.

6.13 The correct answer is: 1, 2 and 3.

The term 'Big Data' describes the storage and analysis of large and/or complex data sets using a range of techniques.

Big Data includes structured and unstructured data, and the technology and techniques used to analyse it.

6.14 The correct answer is: Statement 1 is false but Statement 2 is true.

Big Data enables organisations to leverage complex, unstructured data that was previously ignored because there was no reasonable way to process and analyse it.

To enable this data to be available for analysis requires it to be stored. In the past, computer storage space was relatively constrained. The ability to store vast amounts of data means there are 'big' sets of data available for analysis.

6.15 The correct answer is: Parallel running

This method provides a degree of safety should there be problems with the new system.

Pilot operation involves selecting part or parts of an organisation to operate a new system in parallel with the existing system.

6.16 The correct answers are:

- Training
- Testing
- Conversion

Data flow diagrams and prototyping are techniques used in the system analysis and design stages, not the systems implementation stage.

6.17 The correct answer is: Direct changeover

The key issue here is that the organisation of the business is changing so drastically that the continued operation of the old system is practically impossible, especially since the central warehouse is to be closed as soon as possible. A direct changeover is therefore appropriate.

6.18 The correct answer is: Steps 2, 3, 1, 4

You would need to see the problem first, as it may not be particularly serious, or worthy of a great deal of management time. Then you would wish to ensure that some order was brought into current and future purchasing, and you would lay down organisation-wide standards and so forth. This ensures that the problem is contained and then you can start to plan for the future. Centralisation of capital expenditure authorisation would ensure that the standards are complied with. This is likely to be the most contentious of all. User departments would not wish to see their budgets cut.

6.19 The correct answer is:

- The proposed upgrade does not support TS's strategic requirements because the nature of the product and its manufacturing does not require an elaborate system.

One option can be discounted relatively easily as the new system would not hugely reduce operating costs.

The other options are not as clear cut. The correct answer could be perceived as the **best** answer as the existing system was working fine, and a more elaborate system is not a necessity.

However, there may be some merit in expanding the computer network and collecting production data, and of an information system that gathers external information relating to developments in steel and in uses of steel.

6.20 The correct answers are:

- Contractual flexibility
- Exit route
- Standard of service level required

The SLA needs to address what happens if the agreement needs renegotiating or the circumstances change, therefore flexibility is important to address. Similarly the exit route needs to be agreed so that the organisation is not left without any support at all should the agreement lapse or be broken for any reason. Standard of service level required is the obvious option to be included as this is vital to any outsourcing agreement.

The number of staff is not highly significant as long as the required level of service is met, and is a decision of the outsourcing company, rather than part of the agreement. Also, whilst it is of concern whether the outsourcing company provides services to a company where there might be a conflict of interest, it does not traditionally form part of the agreement. This aspect is usually covered by a confidentiality of information clause. Many outsourcing companies specialise within a business sector so it is likely that a competitor organisation may be using the same outsourcer.

6.21 The correct answers are:

- The volume of data
- The proportion of external data
- The proportion of unstructured data

Big Data differs from earlier approaches in three fundamental ways:

- A higher volume of data
- A higher proportion of external data
- A higher proportion of unstructured data (not fitting neatly into the columns and rows of a database)

Big Data is in digital form, but this is not a change as computerised data was previously in digital form. Big Data is less consistent in type and structure, for example it includes Tweets, images, emails, videos etc.

6.22 The correct answers are:

- B needs to obtain consent to hold sensitive personal data.
- B must supply an individual with a copy of the data held, if asked to do so.
- B should make corrections when told about inaccurate data that it holds.

Under most data protection legislation, companies should not pass on personal data to unauthorised parties. Personal data also should not be retained for longer than it is needed.

Note: the P3 exam will not focus on any one jurisdiction, but in this case, the EU's General Data Protection Regulation has been used as an illustration of data protection legislation. This is consistent with many other jurisdictions.

6.23 The correct answer is:

Assessed through a comparison against short-term financial targets	**Budget constrained**
Assessed through non-budgetary performance measures	**Non-accounting focused**
Focus on the organisation continuing to achieve its overall financial goals	**Profit conscious**

The correct answers reflect the correct definitions of the manager-types.

Even if unfamiliar with this theory, there are clues in the question. In the context of the information provided:

'Overall financial goals' implies 'profit'.

'Non-accounting' implies 'non-budgetary'.

'Constrained' implies 'short-term targets'.

7 Internal Audit

7.1 The correct answers are:

- To set out the audit objectives and the other priorities that apply
- To define how the audit evidence necessary to achieve the objectives will be achieved
- To identify the resources that will be needed and actually employed in audits

7.2 The correct answer is: Comparing financial and non-financial performance with other organisations

The key element of this is the use of the term 'comparing', which is central to effective benchmarking.

7.3 The correct answer is: 3 only.

Internal audit monitors risk strategies to ensure that they operate effectively. Internal audit does not have a part in determining policy or identifying risks. Instead, it monitors what others have put into place and looks at issues of efficiency and effectiveness.

7.4 The correct answer is: It aims to reveal weaknesses in the performance of individual managers and in the overall management structure.

Financial performance would be considered but the audit should cover non-financial issues as well. Assessment of resources is part of the assessment of the adequacy of management structure.

7.5 The correct answers are:

- Establish whether the controls are operating as they are expected to be.
- Establish whether the documentation relating to controls fairly reflects the operation of the system.
- Establish whether improvements need to be made to controls.
- Form an opinion as to the adequacy of the system as a whole for managing the risks identified.

The objectives of tests of controls are similar for internal and external auditors. The purposes for internal auditors include determining whether the controls are operating as they are expected to be, whether the documentation is adequate, whether improvements need to be made, and to form an opinion as to the adequacy of the system as a whole. The identification of persons whose performance is not acceptable may be a by-product of this process, but it is not normally a primary objective.

7.6 The correct answer is: Flag this as a compliance error because part of the purpose of an internal audit is to encourage the application of procedures.

There is no evidence of this being a widespread problem, so further consideration is probably unnecessary. Internal Audit does not usually perform work just so it can be seen to be busy. The compliance test is on the recruitment process, not the quality of their work.

7.7 The correct answers are:

- Check whether the variances are reported within three working days of month end.
- Check whether the 10% figure for exceptional variances is reasonable.
- Check whether managers report reasons for variances and control action taken within one week.

7.8 The correct answer is: To be effective, internal audit should work **independent of** other areas of the organisation.

Part of the role of internal audit is to ensure other areas of the organisation adhere to the system of internal controls. This is best achieved through remaining independent. Working relationships should be professional and civil, but not close.

Working collaboratively and or being closely integrated into other areas of the business would hinder independence.

Internal audit also requires a 'strong voice' and the authority to ensure recommendations are taken seriously. This would not be possible if internal audit was subordinate to other areas of the organisation.

7.9 The correct answer is: Analytical procedures are often used as tests of controls.

Analytical procedures can be used in certain circumstances as an alternative to detailed substantive testing of transactions and balances, where the overall balance examined is immaterial, for example. Analytical procedures can be used as part of risk assessment and at the final review stage - external auditors must use them at these stages as it is required by ISA 315 Identifying and assessing the risks of material misstatement through understanding the entity and its environment and ISA 520 Analytical procedures.

7.10 The correct answer is: Testing the sequence of dispatch notes and enquiring into any missing items

Reviewing sales ledger accounts of individual customers can give assurance that credit limits are not being exceeded but will not demonstrate whether sales to that customer have been completely recorded. Checking that statements are sent out regularly to customers is a check on credit control procedures. Checking items in the sales ledger will confirm that they reflect the original records of sales (the sales day book) but won't confirm that all sales recorded in the sales day book have been recorded in the sales ledger.

7.11 The correct answer is: A misallocation of distribution costs as advertising expenses.

A misallocation of distribution costs as advertising expenses would be picked up by reviewing the statement of profit or loss and other comprehensive income from one year to the next. The other options would not be picked up as there is no corresponding figure in last year's statement of profit or loss to compare against this year's.

7.12 The correct answer is: Errors in computation led to opening inventory being overvalued and the company has also increased sales as a result of a marketing drive based on undercutting competitors.

Undervaluing opening inventory and increasing closing inventory value through indirect overheads would both reduce costs of sales and so increase the gross margin.

Overvaluing the opening inventory would decrease the gross margin - the effect of this would then be cancelled out by the increase in closing inventory value through indirect overheads.

The entry into the market of a major new competitor would reduce sales volumes, but this does not directly translate into a change in the company's gross margin.

Overvaluing the opening inventory, combined with a marketing drive to undercut competitors is the correct answer. Both would have the effect of reducing gross margin.

7.13 The correct answers are:

- Customers are taking longer to pay than they used to.
- Credit terms to receivables have changed.
- The accounting records on which the calculation has been based may be inaccurate.
- Cash received from customers may have been misappropriated.

If customers are taking longer to pay than they used to, receivable days may rise. If credit terms have changed, receivables may be paying more slowly. If the accounting records on which the calculation has been based are inaccurate, receivable days may appear to rise. If cash has been misappropriated, it may appear that receivable days have risen.

If customers are paying more promptly than they used to, receivable days will fall.

7.14 The correct answers are:

- Outsource the internal audit function.
- Ensure the head of internal audit has access to the chair of the board of directors and is accountable to the audit committee.
- Ensure the internal auditors are physically separate from the rest of the workforce.

Working closely with directors creates a familiarity threat, while working in departments which the auditor then goes on to audit could create a self-review threat.

7.15 The correct answer is: Checking movements of inventory from one of the organisation's locations to another

Audit of procurement is audit of the purchasing process. Internal movements of inventory are not connected with purchasing, they are to do with the logistics of operations.

7.16 The correct answer is: Checking that approved sales orders indicate that reference was made to the aged listing.

Reference should be evidenced by signature - checking for that signature is the controls test.

7.17 The correct answer is: To provide an objective estimate of the probability of error in the population

Using statistical sampling cannot reduce the need for judgement in auditing as it is still required to be exercised by the auditor.

Statistical sampling does not reduce the number of items to be tested.

Ensuring that a representative sample is selected is achieved through statistical sampling but is not the main advantage of statistical sampling.

7.18 The correct answers are:

- Analysis of gross operating margins by manufacturing site
- Analysis of wastage by site
- Verifying volumes delivered by each sales agent

Analysing revenue by country is not a priority as cost control and quality standards are mentioned in the scenario as key to maintaining brand leadership.

Advising the production team about the standards used in the company's costing system would not be a priority either, as fluctuations in the cost of ingredients mean that standards will vary, so such an activity is unlikely to add value.

Analysis of gross operating margins by manufacturing site would be seen as a priority given the risk of volatile ingredient costs that could exist across countries.

Similarly, analysis of wastage by site would also be seen to be a priority due to the need to monitor the quality of ingredients which can vary.

Finally, verifying volumes delivered by each sales agent would be a priority as the contract sums paid to agents are dependent on this data being correct (especially in marginal terms if the next 'step' in volumes is achieved, triggering higher contract costs).

7.19 The correct answers are:

- Rationalisation
- Opportunity
- Pressure

Rationalisation, opportunity and pressure are necessary for fraud.

Collusion is sometimes involved in fraud, but fraud is possible without collusion. For example, many frauds are committed by individuals acting alone, taking advantage of weaknesses in control systems.

Complacency helps make fraud easier, but fraud is possible without complacency. For example, if collusion is involved even well-designed control systems can be contravened.

7.20 The correct answers are:

- Review of the number of employees required to achieve a certain amount of work
- Requiring employees being paid cash wages to collect them in person
- Comparison of payroll with employee personnel records

Timesheets will not be an effective control by themselves as there is no guarantee that timesheets submitted will be for genuine employees.

7.21 The correct answers are:

- Checking the adequacy of contingency arrangements
- Reviewing forecasts of future activities

Checking operations on a day-to-day basis and approving the size and nature of transactions are tasks that should be part of the regular control systems and carried out by management. Internal audit should be independent of treasury control systems, observing and not participating.

8 Cybersecurity Threats

8.1 The correct answers are:

- Customer names
- Employee ethnic origin
- Company bank statements
- Employee emails

Company phone numbers are likely to be available on the company's website, while the company's bank details are likely to be available on bills or invoices.

8.2 The correct answer is: Availability

Availability means accessible, but only to those with the right to have it, for legitimate purposes only (ie objectives for opening it up).

Confidentiality means ensuring that legitimately available data is protected from unauthorised access (ie objectives for closing it off).

Integrity of data means accurate, intelligible, reliable, not lost, not corrupted.

Integrity of processing means not used for illegal or immoral purposes, not used in a way that the data subject did not intend.

8.3 The correct answers are:

- Social proof
- Authority
- Reciprocation

Here are the six influences cited in Cialdini's work:

1. Reciprocation - the desire to repay a good deed done to them
2. Commitment and consistency - avoiding being seen as a hypocrite
3. Social proof - mimicking the behaviour of others around us in uncertain situations
4. Liking - people tend to behave in the same way as the people they like
5. Authority - people will also obey and instruction from someone who is in charge
6. Scarcity - a shortage of something can make it more important

Imitation may refer to the same principle as social proof, but the term is not used in Cialdini's work. Similarly, plausibility is a combination of social proof and authority but is not a recognised term from his work either.

8.4 The correct answer is: External expertise on cybersecurity

External expertise on cybersecurity is required to ensure an informed policy decision is made.

Budgets for implementation are important for determining parameters, but form part of the objectives themselves, not the process.

Appointment of a chief information officer will be an output of the process once the objectives have been set.

Benchmarking with other similar organisations is a plausible option, but is more likely to be part of the overall objectives, not the process itself.

8.5 The correct answers are:

- Internet
- Website

Internet is used to stay connected to suppliers, while the website is used for retail operations. An intranet is only used internally, so would not be used for retail operations. Phone is not used for retail either. Social media may be useful for gathering and monitoring customer feedback, but it is not precise and is not used for retail operations.

8.6 The correct answer is: Company Y faces cybersecurity threats from both its technology and its delivery channels.

Company Y faces cybersecurity threats from both its technology and its delivery channels because email (its delivery channel) can contain cybersecurity threats, such as malware, which could be installed on the PC (its technology).

8.7 The correct answer is: Viruses

This new system is at risk because of viruses from students using other devices at home which the school would not previously have been in contact with.

Hacking, ransomware and phishing are not new risks, as the school already receives emails, so these threats will already exist (these are also likely to be actively sent to an entity, whereas a virus can be transmitted without the student knowing).

8.8 The correct answers are:

- Financial
- Legal

Financial risk would arise from damage to PCs from not maintaining controls which may require expensive rectification. Legal risk may occur as T may lose personal data which could lead to litigation if this is in breach of data protection legislation.

Reputation risks would not occur here, as cybersecurity does not affect its reputation as an engineering company.

Commercial risks will not be affected as this will not affect its ability to manufacture and sell goods (the scenario does not mention how dependent T is on technology to make and sell its products). Social risks are also unlikely, as they will not affect T's relationships with stakeholders.

8.9 The correct answer is: Replacing the network cables with wireless technology to maintain contact with each sensor

Replacing the network cables with wireless technology to maintain contact with each sensor does reduce the risk of damage to cables, but creates a cybersecurity risk as the network could now be hacked.

Screening all new employees with access to the DCS for links to terrorist organisations will not have the most significant effect as terrorism is not the only reason to maintain cybersecurity.

Introducing a planned maintenance programme for inspecting pipelines, sensors and cables won't stop any cybersecurity threats.

Increasing the frequency that the DCS anti-virus software is updated from monthly to weekly will have some effect, but not enough, as risks can change on even an hourly basis.

8.10 The correct answer is:

Spear phishing	**Targeting an individual instead of an entire population**
Smishing	**Using text messages**
Vishing	**The use of telephone calls**

Extorting money by blocking access to files or systems until a fee is paid is known as ransomware, while disabling a system by bombarding it with more activity than it can cope with is known as a distributed denial of service (DDoS) attack.

8.11 The correct answer is: Cybersecurity risk

Cybersecurity risk is the most significant risk here, via sabotage from ex-employees with technical knowledge who may still hold a grudge against Company Q.

There is no evidence to suggest that reputation risk would occur here. Financial risk is also unlikely, as the service employs fewer staff so is probably cheaper now. There should be no litigation risk as the VR process was followed appropriately.

8.12 The correct answers are:

- Malware from students
- Malware from hackers
- Malware from non-teaching staff

Malware from students could be a risk via student emails from any infected external PCs that are sent to tutors whose own PCs could then be used to access the private system.

Malware from hackers could access the private system locally as it is wireless.

Malware from non-teaching staff is also a risk, as they are given access to the private network and could be targeted by malware.

Malware is least likely from visitors to the campus as they are not given access to the private network.

8.13 The correct answers are:

- Infected memory sticks
- Unauthorised websites accessed by staff
- Illegally obtained software
- Employees with a grudge against the organisation

Hacking, ransomware and spyware all originate from outside of the organisation.

8.14 The correct answers are:

- Firewalls
- Monitoring software

Contingency planning would be too late to stop a cybersecurity risk from happening, as would appointing an information officer and taking legal action.

8.15 The correct answer is: Hacking

Ransomware is where access to sensitive data is withheld unless a payment is made.

Phishing is where an email address, password and credit card details have been obtained by a third party pretending to be a legitimate contact.

Distributed denial of service attack is where online operations have been suspended due to excessive amounts of false enquiries which the system cannot cope with.

8.16 The correct answer is: an attack which uses an innocent third party's website to host a cyber-attack.

An attack which uses an innocent third party's website to host a cyber-attack is known as a cross-site scripting (XSS) attack.

An attack where data can be accessed via legitimate access to a company's website is known as a structured query language (SQL) injection.

Restricting access to data unless some form of payment is made to the cyber-attacker is better known as ransomware.

Buffer overflow attacks are when a system is bombarded with more data than it can handle. This is a form of DDoS attack.

8.17 The correct answers are:

- Anti-virus software
- Filters against malware
- User education

The appointment of a chief information officer is not relevant. As the name suggests, threat monitoring software monitors but does not defend against attacks. Cybersecurity risk assessment identifies threats but does not defend against them.

8.18 The correct answer is: Exploiting gaps in cybersecurity for their own purposes

Ethical hackers identify gaps in cybersecurity so they can be addressed before they create a threat.

Grey hat hackers offer to fix a cybersecurity threat for a fee but may post the weakness online if the offer is not taken up.

Social engineering is exploiting someone's trust to gain illegal access to personal data.

8.19 The correct answer is: Offering to fix a cybersecurity threat for a fee or posting the weakness online if the offer is not taken up

Unethical hackers exploit gaps in cybersecurity for their own purposes.

Ethical hackers identify gaps in cybersecurity so they can be addressed before they create a threat.

Social engineering is exploiting someone's trust to gain illegal access to personal data.

8.20 The correct answers are:

- Opportunity cost from lost revenue
- Fines and penalties from data regulators

Opportunity cost from lost revenue occurs as IP was stolen which would otherwise have attracted revenue.

Loss of share price is not relevant here as X is a private company.

Increased production costs are also not relevant here, as costs will need to increase to improve cybersecurity.

9 Cybersecurity Processes

9.1 The correct answer is:

Procedures implemented after the cause of the breakdown has been discovered or corrected	**Recovery**
Procedures that ensure that some operations can be performed during the period that normal services are disrupted	**Standby**
Policies to ensure that the recovery plan is implemented and operates as intended	**Personnel**

This is another question that it is possible to answer correctly without specialist knowledge.

'After the cause of the breakdown' implies recovery.

'During the period that normal services are disrupted' implies standby.

'To ensure the recovery plan is implemented' implies personnel.

9.2 The correct answer is:

- Re-use the infrastructure that will be replaced at the current disaster recovery location at a cost of $0.25 million.

Although continuing with the existing recovery facility is the cheapest option, it seems inefficient to dispose of the old system when it can be used as a disaster recovery system at relatively low cost. The benefit would be that the disaster recovery system has been updated.

Having a disaster recovery site more locally is not necessarily beneficial. Disasters may happen locally, for example, natural disasters. F Co does not want to find that both sites have been subject to the same disaster. This is also a very expensive option.

Installing a second system at head office increases the risk of a single disaster impacting both systems.

9.3 The correct answers are:

- Personnel management
- Standby procedures
- Recovery procedures

It should include definitions of responsibilities, priorities, backup and standby arrangements, communications with staff, measures to deal with public relations, and a risk assessment. The other two options are relevant to security: firewalls are used to protect computer systems from viruses and hacking; and physical access control aims to control human access.

9.4 The correct answers are:

- Establishing, maintaining and communicating integrity and ethical values
- Providing board oversight

A cybersecurity governance structure is one which ensures that the organisation has a formal, codified policy statement which outlines its cybersecurity aims and objectives, and has the full approval of its board.

Training and a policy on cybersecurity suppliers are not related to governance: they are more practical and found within cybersecurity risk management processes.

9.5 The correct answers are:

- Service level agreements (SLAs)
- Key performance indicators (KPIs)
- Accreditation using ISO 27001

Having a sponsor at board level is too high up the organisation for such a decision to be taken, while entering into cybersecurity partnership with another organisation may create confidentiality issues with each organisation's data.

9.6 The correct answer is: Man in the middle attack

Man in the middle (MitM) attacks occur when two organisations communicate with each other, but a third party is intercepting their transmissions without their knowledge in order to gain some advantage (in this case, G is using this approach to understand the position required to offer terms of trade that are better than those currently in place between K and E).

Phishing refers to the theft of access details for some kind of personal gain. Social engineering is an approach using some form of deception to allow such access. Malvertising is an advert that appears innocent but which secretly contains harmful malware.

9.7 The correct answer is: Intranet

Service level agreements (SLAs) are generally used with external parties such as contractors, not staff. Liaison officers implies an external link, not one for internal users. Contracts are too formal for a policy that only internal staff would use.

9.8 The correct answer is: Malware

User education is one of the key controls in the fight against social engineering, but anti-virus software is unlikely to protect an organisation from this threat. Similarly, the remaining options are unlikely to be protected by the use of firewalls. Malware is therefore the most appropriate answer here.

9.9 The correct answers are:

- List of responsible staff
- Business continuity arrangements
- Communications protocols

Budget allocations would be too specific to see in this plan, while insurance details would only be required once the scale of the damage is known.

9.10 The correct answer is: Encryption

One of the key uses of the blockchain is to record digital transactions in cryptocurrency, which requires complex mathematical problems to be solved in order to allow access but which uses encryption technology to be considered secure.

Patch management refers to the process of fixing a known cybersecurity problem, often via a software update. A firewall is a barrier to limit access to sensitive data. Back-ups are copies of important data that can be used to restore records in the event of any disruption to systems.

9.11 The correct answers are:

- Controls that preserve data and systems integrity
- Purchasing legitimate software from reputable suppliers

Recruitment of an information officer might help, but is not specifically relevant to these risks and appointing this individual may be too much for a small company.

Introducing secure cloud computing for all data storage is recognised as cybersecurity best practice, but is not relevant to networks or software.

9.12 The correct answer is: Security information and event management

Security information and event management (SIEM) monitors data activity for patterns which could indicate cybersecurity threats. Other teams then act on this intelligence.

Insider threat teams attempt to intercept internal threats.

Threat intelligence teams attempt to intercept external threats.

Hunt teams seek out as yet unidentified cybersecurity breaches.

Incident response teams deal with the immediate aftermath of any breach and are generally known as either computer incident response teams (CIRTs) or computer security incident response teams (CSIRTs).

9.13 The correct answers are:

- Apply consistent methodology for cybersecurity across the organisation
- Apply TARA approach to determine how to manage risks
- Assessment of statement of applicability by accredited auditor

Demonstrating compliance with the GDPR is probably a desired outcome of getting ISO 27001 certified, but is not part of the process.

Obtaining assurance for customers that cybersecurity is effective is also a desired outcome, not part of the process.

9.14 The correct answer is: Internal audit

Internal audit is not specific to cybersecurity so is not relevant here.

9.15 The correct answer is: ISO 27001 accreditation by an external provider

ISO 27001 accreditation by an external provider: size is no barrier and ISO 27001 accreditation is not excessive, plus internal expertise in cyber is unlikely to exist, so this is the best option for Y.

No organisation is exempt from data protection legislation, so having no need for cybersecurity is clearly wrong.

Reports from an internal auditor or the Chief Information Officer are not mentioned (plus the use of these is unlikely for an organisation of this size).

9.16 The correct answer is: Request suitable updates to its cybersecurity to stop the malware from affecting its systems

Informing regulators within 72 hours should be done (eg this is what the EU's GDPR requires) but is not going to correct the issues that led to the breach occurring in the first place.

Taking legal action against the outsourced cybersecurity function will not correct the issues that led to the breach occurring and is unlikely to be successful as it was a new type of malware.

Reviewing the affected data subjects and informing them of the breach should be done, but again, is not going to correct the issues that led to the breach occurring in the first place.

9.17 The correct answers are:

- Reports to board or senior management
- The requirement to inform data protection regulators

A reduction in share price and reputation risk may be associated impacts but are not outputs of the monitoring system.

Resignation of the Risk Manager: events may not be anyone's fault, so resignation would not necessarily be appropriate.

ANSWERS

10 Cybersecurity Tools, Techniques and Reporting

10.1 The correct answer is: The analysis will identify the source and intent of the malware and determine the consequences of the breach.

Identifying the source and intent of the malware and determining the consequences of the breach matches the purposes of forensics: to determine cause, culprits and consequences. None of the other options does this.

10.2 The correct answer is: Converting binary code into source code for the purposes of responding to a malware threat

Breaking binary code apart for the purposes of responding to a malware threat is reverse engineering.

Converting binary code into assembler code for the purposes of responding to a malware threat is disassembly. Breaking binary code apart for the purposes of creating a malware threat is not part of cybersecurity so is clearly incorrect!

10.3 The correct answers are:

- Social engineering
- Defragmentation

Social engineering is the use of deception or other means to illegally access data. Defragmentation is reorganising files on a computer to improve its storage capability.

The remaining options are techniques that are used to respond to malware.

10.4 The correct answer is: Probing a system as part of cybersecurity testing to expose vulnerabilities that can be addressed

Exploiting someone's trust to gain illegal access to personal data is social engineering.

Exploiting gaps in cybersecurity for your own purposes is known as unethical hacking.

Converting binary code into source code for the purposes of responding to a malware threat is decompilation.

10.5 The correct answer is: As part of cybersecurity testing when looking for exploitable vulnerabilities

Determining the cause, culprits and consequences of malware is forensic testing.

Identifying gaps in cybersecurity so they can be addressed before they create a threat is ethical hacking (similar to penetration testing, but less proactive).

Cyber risk reporting frameworks include SOC for Cybersecurity or SOC 2 for external organisations.

10.6 The correct answer is: BYOD policy

BYOD or 'bring your own device' policies specify the minimum standards of software security that an employee would need in order to use their own device at work.

SOC for cybersecurity offers external accreditation for overall cybersecurity, while SOC 2 covers external accreditation for overall cybersecurity in outsource organisations.

ISO 31000 is a risk management standard - if you selected this, you may have been confusing it with ISO 27001 which does relate to cybersecurity standards.

10.7 The correct answers are:

- Leadership roles for cybersecurity
- Officers responsible for making cybersecurity decisions
- Feedback on cybersecurity events
- Links between cybersecurity objectives and organisational objectives

Cybersecurity budgets and vendor due diligence are more useful for managers, not board members.

10.8 The correct answers are:

- Number of cybersecurity breaches in last six months
- Details of SOC 2 accreditation

The average time taken to process the payroll and benchmark data against other payroll providers both relate to payroll, not cybersecurity, so would not be in this list.

SOC for cybersecurity accreditation is not used for outsource organisations: SOC 2 should be followed.

10.9 The correct answers are:

- A description of the cybersecurity system used by management
- Assertions made by management about the cybersecurity controls in place
- An opinion by a CPA that the controls in place were effective

An assessment of the controls in a service organisation and a list of the detailed tests carried out by the CPA would be found in a SOC 2 report.

SOC for cybersecurity reports are generally widely available, while SOC 2 report distribution is usually limited.

10.10 The correct answers are:

- An opinion by a CPA that the description in the assertion matches the AICPA trust services criteria
- An opinion by a CPA that the controls in place were effective
- Assertions made by service organisation management about the description of controls

A description of the cybersecurity system used by management would be found in a SOC for cybersecurity report. The criteria used must be AICPA trust services criteria, not those suggested by management.

Practice mock questions

1 Questions

1 **Match the following definitions with the correct risk classification terms from the pull down list options below:**

An event or events from which either good or bad outcomes could occur

[▼]

A risk whose only possible outcome can be harmful

[▼]

A risk that affects people in general which cannot be controlled by individuals

[▼]

Pull down list:

Fundamental
Speculative risk
Pure risk

---

2 X is a company that distributes a range of different types of films to cinemas across many countries throughout the world. In most cases, they have entered into a contract with the producers of each film to run advertising campaigns and ensure that films are shown in cinemas in line with a pre-arranged release strategy. Occasionally X will distribute its own films. X also distributes and markets films for home rental via DVD and Blu-ray discs on behalf of producers once the law in each country allows it.

Which of the following are strategic risks to X?

Select ALL that apply.

☐ A fall in the population's disposable income

☐ Digital piracy

☐ Downloads to TVs, PCs and other digital devices

☐ Showing movies in 3D as well as 2D

☐ Demographic change within a country

---

3 Y is an airline that operates domestic and international flights and employs cabin crew who, among other duties, are responsible for delivering a safety demonstration to passengers that explains what they should do in the event of a crash landing. This includes the use of emergency exits, floor-level lighting and lifejackets stored under each passenger's seat.

Which of the following risks is Y attempting to manage by delivering the safety demonstration?

Select ALL that apply.

☐ Legal risk

☐ Reputation risk

☐ Litigation risk

☐ Human hazard risk

☐ Employee risk

---

4 B is a bank that pays interest to savers at a rate matching the base rate in its country, Z, which is currently 0.5% per annum (pa) on deposits of $100 million. Across the whole of country Z, there is pressure to change interest rates in an attempt to address economic issues - however, opinion is equally divided over whether rates should be raised or lowered. B's finance department has suggested that if rates were to rise to 0.75% pa, deposits would rise to $150 million, but if rates were to fall to 0.25% pa, deposits would fall to $70 million. Currently the finance department believes that either option is equally likely, but as Z's largest bank, there is concern that if B's rates were changed from the current amount, this may send out the wrong message to investors and affect confidence.

The board of B has agreed to consider the impact of any changes on interest payable to investors and will lobby the government of Z either way - however, it is keen to consider the option that returns the lowest amount of interest to investors.

From the following list of options, select the most appropriate action:

○ Keep rates at 0.5%

○ Lobby the government to change rates

○ Need more information

---

5 'The assets that allow an organisation to take risks and absorb losses.'

Which ONE of the following options is the term used to describe the statement above?

○ Risk capacity

○ Risk appetite

○ Risk attitude

○ Risk approach

---

6 ISO 31000 *Risk Management* is a standardised approach to risk management. It contains a series of principles, a framework for implementing these principles and an iterative process for managing risk.

From the following list, identify which ones are included in the risk management principles within ISO 31000 *Risk Management*.

Select ALL that apply.

☐ Aligned with all other activities

☐ A commitment to risk management

☐ Embedded within the organisation

☐ Limitations in available information actively considered

☐ Recording and reporting

☐ Continual improvement through learning and experience

---

7 B is a motor manufacturer that operates a just-in-time system of inventory supply for all its components. Each supplier has a contract to supply B with a series of specific components that must be fulfilled within a set timescale. The contract states that if any supplier cannot meet this timescale or specification, B can source appropriate components from another supplier without affecting price or supply.

Which ONE of the following risk responses using the TARA framework is most likely to equate to the way that B has addressed its component risk?

○ Accept

○ Reduce

○ Transfer

○ Avoid

---

8 C is a mining company that extracts precious metals for use in the telecommunications industry from a variety of different locations across the world. Some of these locations have presented different levels of risk to others, requiring a formal risk management approach to address such volatility. C's policy has always been to manage risks in the following order of priority:

1 Maintaining human life
2 Ensuring legal behaviour
3 Maintaining shareholder value
4 Respecting environmental responsibility

C has mining operations in Country P where a problem has recently arisen. A new government has been formed which has taken a very hostile view of any overseas investment, especially those where national assets are at stake. It has passed a new law in P allowing the government to reclaim land on which such mines are based, by force if necessary, and claim any mineral reserves in the national interest of P. C's lawyers believe that the government in P is likely to agree to a financial settlement in lieu of this action, although they estimate that it will need to be a significant settlement to protect the mine from any further action. Until now, the mine in P was the most profitable site operated by C.

Assuming that C is not risk averse, select which ONE of the options listed below that C would be most likely to use in response to these events.

○ Vacate the mine immediately and allow the government of P to seize all assets

○ Pay the fine immediately and continue to work on the mine

○ Pay the fine immediately but remove all workers until it is deemed safe

○ Do nothing and lobby the international community to support C by highlighting the contract drawn up between C and the original government of P

---

9 **Which TWO of the following are organisational levels in the COSO Internal Control - Integrated Framework (or cube)?**

☐ Entity level

☐ Division

☐ Department

☐ Company

---

10 Consider the following risk responses made by five different organisations.

In each case, select which ONE of the four TARA options the organisation has adopted (note that each TARA option may be used more than once or not at all).

1 D is a campsite that posts notices for guests around its swimming pool that no lifeguards are on duty. [▼]

2 E is an estate agency that has closed 10% of its branches due to a fiercely competitive sales environment. [▼]

3 F is a doctor's surgery that sends its entire medical staff on regular and frequent training courses to improve their medical treatment skills. [▼]

4 G is a nation that operates a space exploration programme and launches manned rockets four times a year to carry out experiments in zero gravity. [▼]

5 H is a supermarket that has recently suffered damage to its reputation due to errors in product labelling. As a result of this scandal, H has now changed suppliers for all affected products. [▼]

Pull down list:

Transfer
Avoid
Reduce
Accept

---

11 **From the following statements made by individuals within an organisation, state whether they display behaviour that is risk seeking, risk averse or if it is impossible to tell.**

1 'I don't care about the costs, we need to increase throughput as much as possible to meet demand!' [▼]

2 'I'm not happy with this course of action as the outcome does not match the effort required to achieve it.' [▼]

3 'My advice is to accept this course of action as that's what we did last year.' [▼]

4 'Considering the returns from this new product, I think we should explore the costs associated with it further.' [▼]

Pull down list:

Risk seeker
Risk averse
Impossible to tell

---

12 Consider the following definition:

'The risk remaining after actions have been taken to manage risks.'

Which of the following types of risk is this statement describing?

- ○ Gross risk
- ○ Residual risk
- ○ Balloon risk
- ○ Post-response risk

---

13 **Which of the following remuneration methods may be used to align the interests of directors (agents) with those of shareholders (principals)?**

Select ALL that apply.

- ☐ High basic salary
- ☐ Profit-related pay
- ☐ Shares
- ☐ Executive pension scheme contributions
- ☐ Executive share option plans

---

14 **Which ONE of the following would NOT normally be a role fulfilled by the chair of a company?**

- ○ Ensuring the board receives accurate and timely information
- ○ Leading the induction programme for new directors
- ○ Being responsible for developing new investment initiatives
- ○ Facilitating board appraisal
- ○ Helping to promote understanding of the views of directors

---

15 **Which of the following would NOT be regarded as good practice for the nomination committee?**

Select ALL that apply.

- ☐ The nomination committee should consider the need to attract board members from a diversity of backgrounds.
- ☐ The nomination committee should consist entirely of executive directors.
- ☐ The nomination committee should regularly review the structure, size and composition of the board.
- ☐ The nomination committee should consider whether non-executive directors are spending enough time on their duties.
- ☐ The nomination committee should use an external search consultancy and open advertising when recruiting a chair.

---

16 **In the context of corporate governance, which ONE of the following concepts can be defined as meaning straightforward and honest?**

- ○ Independence
- ○ Objectivity
- ○ Transparency
- ○ Integrity
- ○ Responsibility

---

17 MM works as a senior member of the accounts department of BG Co. Recently he has carried out investment appraisal calculations on the development of a major new product. Because his boss was away on holiday, MM checked the calculations himself and signed them off as satisfactory.

From the following list of threats to MM's independence as an accountant, select which ONE best matches the circumstances described above.

- ○ Self-interest
- ○ Advocacy
- ○ Familiarity
- ○ Self-review

---

18 **Which ONE of the following is least likely to be a problem when an organisation attempts to enforce its ethical code?**

- ○ The code is perceived by staff as inflexible.
- ○ The code does not deal with the ethical problems that employees encounter in practice.
- ○ Senior managers regularly act contrary to the code.
- ○ There are no disciplinary measures in place to deal with any employees who breach the code.

---

19 Company J has decided to implement COSO's Enterprise Risk Management: Integrating with Strategy and Performance (2017) into its approach to managing risks. It has set a risk appetite, assessed its risks, implemented a feedback loop to assess its performance and shares this via the company's intranet.

Which ONE of the following is an element of the COSO approach that Company J has NOT yet adopted?

- ○ Strategy and objective setting
- ○ Performance
- ○ Review and revision
- ○ Governance and culture
- ○ Information, communication and reporting

---

20 **Which TWO of the following are designated responsibilities of an organisation's risk manager?**

- ☐ Establishing a common risk management language
- ☐ Setting the organisation's risk appetite
- ☐ Providing leadership, vision and direction for enterprise risk management
- ☐ Deciding the board's approach towards enterprise risk management

---

21 Which issues from the following list represent environmental and/or social issues for a manufacturer of fast-moving consumer goods?

Select ALL that apply.

- ☐ The materials used in manufacture
- ☐ The price charged in different markets
- ☐ The risk a competitor product will provide superior performance
- ☐ The employment conditions in supplier workplaces
- ☐ The packaging used

---

22 Despite the various approaches to corporate governance in use across the world, the relationship between audit committees and external auditors tends to display a number of key themes.

Which of the following roles and responsibilities relating to the external auditor would you expect to see in the terms of reference for an audit committee?

Select ALL that apply.

- ☐ Remuneration arrangements
- ☐ The provision of non-audit services
- ☐ Assessment of objectivity and independence
- ☐ Communicating errors in the draft financial statements
- ☐ Assessment of the control environment
- ☐ Determining the organisation's risk appetite

---

23 Company A is an online retailer selling a wide variety of products across many different countries. It has pursued a cost leadership strategy allowing it to offer extremely competitive prices. It has also developed a digital infrastructure that includes sales via its website alongside supplier management and fulfilment systems in operation at its distribution centres. Company A's customer service is generally considered to be excellent. However, media reports in many countries have also suggested that Company A's employees suffer poor treatment in the workplace, which has pushed a number of consumers towards other retailers instead.

Which of the following statements is MOST accurate when describing the impact that A's strategy has had on its brand?

- ○ Products are more easily available at a cheaper price than using other online retailers.
- ○ Products can be ordered using the website 24/7.
- ○ Products are cheapest on A's website.
- ○ Buying products from A means you agree with their values.

---

24 Company C is a global soft drinks manufacturer which has been criticised for promoting unsafe working practices at some of its bottling plants and diverting water supplies from vulnerable communities to manufacture some of its products. Both of these allegations against Company C have surfaced in developing countries where health and safety standards are not as strict as they are in its home country.

Which ONE of the following risks is the company most likely to face as a result of these events?

- ○ Adverse reputation risk
- ○ Increased litigation risk in the developing countries
- ○ Adverse impact on the company's supply chain
- ○ Overspend on its advertising budgets

---

25 **Which TWO of the following terms would you expect to see when considering stress-testing in the banking industry?**

- ☐ Dodd-Frank
- ☐ Basel III
- ☐ Sarbanes-Oxley
- ☐ ISO 31000

---

26 Company F is an international motor manufacturer which exports its cars to many countries. The board of Company F is debating the investment it should be making to counter the many technological disruptions currently present in the automotive industry.

Which THREE of the following disruptions should the board of Company F be most concerned about as part of this debate?

- ☐ Shortage of fossil fuels
- ☐ Raw material prices
- ☐ Changes in government legislation
- ☐ Over-capacity in its production facilities
- ☐ Rise of electric and hybrid engines
- ☐ International trade tariffs

---

27 Company A specialises in shelving and other storage solutions for CDs, DVDs and Blu-ray discs. Previously, Company A has been the market leader but sales are now declining. The directors of Company A decide that to address this situation, they will continue with their existing strategy and increase production of its existing ranges of shelving.

Which of the following BEST describes the risks associated with this strategy?

- ○ Customer demand will put pressure on A's production capacity
- ○ The extra marketing spend will have a detrimental impact on profits
- ○ Additional market research testing will affect profits
- ○ The investment may not deliver the required returns

---

28 Company H is a retailer of CDs, DVDs, Blu-rays and other entertainment items. Most of its products are also sold online and by other larger retailers. It operates from a series of retail locations in one country and has a recognised brand name for its stores. It has recently reported falling sales which many in the industry are blaming on the disruption caused by digital technology and the way that consumers access music and movies.

Which ONE of the following disruptions to H's current strategy is most likely to have caused this decline?

○ Competition from online retailers of CDs, DVDs and Blu-rays

○ Inability to sell via its own app or website

○ Increasing demand for streaming

○ Illegal copies of CDs, DVDs and Blu-rays

---

29 **Which TWO of the following techniques would an organisation be most likely to use when stress testing its resources in the event of a planned new product launch?**

☐ Sensitivity analysis

☐ Value at risk

☐ Net present value

☐ Payback

---

30 Company C is a construction company working on significant public sector projects such as the construction of hospitals and bridges.

Which of the following assumptions are most relevant to Company C and its strategy?

Select ALL that apply.

☐ Economic uncertainty

☐ Change in government

☐ Consumer tastes changing

☐ Increase in digital technology

---

31 **Which of the following types of information is MOST susceptible to cybersecurity risk due to its sensitivity?**

Select ALL that apply.

☐ Customer date of birth

☐ Customer email address

☐ Company address

☐ Employee pay details

☐ Employee addresses

☐ Company registration details

---

32 **Which ONE of the following types of information is LEAST susceptible to cybersecurity risk due to its sensitivity?**

- ○ Company products
- ○ Customer addresses
- ○ Customer phone numbers
- ○ Customer payment history
- ○ Customer credit card details

---

33 Company T is determining what its cybersecurity objectives should be for a variety of areas of its operations. One of the draft objectives states that legitimately available data is protected from unauthorised access.

Which ONE of the following categories does this objective refer to?

- ○ Availability
- ○ Confidentiality
- ○ Integrity of data
- ○ Integrity of processing

---

34 **Which of the following is a cybersecurity opportunity created by ethical hackers?**

- ○ Exploiting gaps in cybersecurity for their own purposes
- ○ Identifying gaps in cybersecurity so they can be addressed before they create a threat
- ○ Exploiting someone's trust to gain illegal access to personal data
- ○ Offering to fix a cybersecurity threat for a fee or posting the weakness online if the offer is not taken up

---

35 **Which of the following would be considered an external threat arising from malware?**

Select ALL that apply.

- ☐ Ransomware
- ☐ Hacking
- ☐ Unauthorised websites accessed by staff
- ☐ Illegally obtained software
- ☐ Infected memory sticks
- ☐ Employees with a grudge against the organisation
- ☐ Spyware

---

36 Consider the following job description from an employee of an organisation. 'I work within a part of the business that is responsible for cybersecurity. My team is specifically responsible for seeking threats that have not yet been identified.'

Which ONE of the following terms BEST describes the part of the business where this employee works?

- ○ Insider threat team
- ○ Threat intelligence team
- ○ Hunt team
- ○ Incident response team

---

37 **Which of the following terms BEST describes reverse engineering?**

- ○ Converting binary code into assembler code for the purposes of responding to a malware threat
- ○ Breaking binary code apart for the purposes of responding to a malware threat
- ○ Converting binary code into source code for the purposes of responding to a malware threat
- ○ Breaking binary code into separate streams to allow more than one person to analyse it

---

38 An individual has suffered a cybersecurity breach from a web application attack where their email address, password and credit card details have been obtained by a third party pretending to be a legitimate contact.

Which of the following terms does this description relate to?

- ○ Hacking
- ○ Ransomware
- ○ Phishing
- ○ Distributed denial of service attack

---

39 Company F has developed a cybersecurity policy to include objectives, expectations, responsibilities and related matters which it needs to communicate to both internal and external users of this policy. This includes its legal responsibilities as part of recently introduced legislation designed to secure any personal data collected and stored during normal business activities.

Which ONE of the following techniques would be the MOST appropriate technique for Company F to educate external users?

- ○ Service level agreement (SLA)
- ○ Intranet
- ○ Workplace learning
- ○ Face-to-face meetings

---

40 Company B has implemented a cybersecurity program that uses externally purchased software and hardware in conjunction with a third-party data processing company and external cloud computing for data storage.

Which TWO of the following techniques would Company B find most useful when identifying, assessing and managing the risks associated with its cybersecurity vendors and business partners?

- ☐ Due diligence
- ☐ Employing an external law firm to select each
- ☐ Contracts
- ☐ Having a sponsor at board level
- ☐ Obtaining references from other customers

---

41 An organisation is looking to implement ISO 27001 accredited responses to manage its cybersecurity threats.

Which ONE of the following controls would you NOT expect to find within the ISO 27001 recommended control sets?

- ○ Organisation of information security (managing mobile devices and BYOD policies)
- ○ Information committee
- ○ Asset management
- ○ Cryptography (including encryption)
- ○ Communications security (including networks and telecoms)
- ○ Information security incident management (monitoring, detecting and responding to security events)

---

42 Company H is a supplier of health and beauty products to supermarkets and other retailers. It operates an online e-commerce system which helps to manage its suppliers and allows customers to order and pay for goods. Company H suspects that the e-commerce system has suffered a cybersecurity breach and intends to use forensic analysis to investigate the suspected breach.

Which ONE of the following statements BEST describes the use of forensic analysis to investigate the suspected breach at Company H?

- ○ The analysis will determine whether a breach has occurred and confirm the cause, culprits and consequences.
- ○ The analysis will determine the cause, culprits and consequences of the breach.
- ○ The analysis will determine whether a breach has occurred and confirm the consequences.
- ○ The analysis will confirm the extent of the breach by analysing the malware to identify its source.

---

43 **Which of the following items would be examined when using strategic management accounting?**

Select ALL that apply.

- ☐ Market share
- ☐ Brand values
- ☐ Competitor profitability
- ☐ Cash flow
- ☐ New entrants in the market

---

44 Company Q is a manufacturer of products that are designed to help people stop smoking, such as patches, gum and some types of e-cigarettes. The following categories of performance measurement are used by the senior management team to ensure the company meets its targets: quality, delivery, process time and flexibility.

From the following sources of data, select the most likely category of performance that Q is attempting to measure from the list of pull-down options below (some categories may be used more than once or not at all).

Overtime paid to machine operatives [▼]

Complaints from customers [▼]

Complaints from retailers [▼]

Machine downtime [▼]

Pull down list:

Quality
Delivery
Process time
Flexibility

---

45 Organisations which frequently use short-term performance measures to justify an action sometimes fail to understand the longer-term implications of these actions.

From the following responses to recognised performance issues, match them to the most likely adverse implication from the pull-down list of options below.

Buying in bulk to address adverse price variances [▼]

Additional production to improve labour efficiency [▼]

Product re-working to reduce the percentage of products failing final quality checks

[▼]

Pull down list:

Adverse inventory holding costs
Adverse productivity levels
Adverse inventory amounts

---

46 R works as a reporting accountant for an agro-chemical company and helps to prepare the monthly 'board pack' for directors and other information for major stakeholders such as lenders and regulators. As part of her role, she also supports the finance director with advice on methods that could streamline the reporting process and allow better decision making.

She has produced a series of recommendations for the next board pack that includes a number of initiatives she feels the board could benefit from, but the finance director feels they should be explained more fully and has suggested a brief summary of each one that explains their purpose and benefit.

From the following list of descriptions, identify the most likely form of reporting initiative that is being proposed from the pull-down list of options below.

'An efficient system that helps avoid information overload by highlighting key information only, usually by setting parameters from which management action is likely to be required, such as overspending which exceeds budget by 5%.' [▼]

'This is an enhancement to our existing reporting structure that allows users to start with a macro view of our entire business and then focus on specific key areas by applying more of a micro-approach to a variety of activities.' [▼]

'The starting point for all users, showing all activity and performance in a summarised and sometimes graphical manner, supported by financial and non-financial information sourced from a variety of parts of the company.' [▼]

Pull down list:

Full cost accounting report
Executive dashboard
Drill down report
Balanced scorecard
Exception reporting

---

47 **For each of the following control systems based around rewards, identify whether they are likely to be considered effective or ineffective for the organisation described:**

Performance-related pay for an executive director of a retailer where performance is based on market share and sales targets. [▼]

A discretionary bonus paid to air traffic controllers for ensuring all flights take off from the airport where they are based on schedule. [▼]

A manufacturer of mobile telecommunication processors employs quality control inspectors who run a specialised test on a sample of processors from each production run. Inspectors are paid a basic salary plus a variable amount for each faulty item identified.

[▼]

Pull down list:

Effective
Ineffective

---

48 **Which of the following factors are NOT part of the control environment of an organisation?**

Select ALL that apply.

- ☐ The directors' operating style
- ☐ The structure of authority showing segregation of duties and supervision
- ☐ Methods of imposing control used by directors, such as internal audit
- ☐ A code of conduct for all employees to sign up to
- ☐ A procedures manual for paying wages and salaries

---

49 Company S has adopted a structure where controls are split into separate activities for review by different specialist staff from the company's internal audit team. One such area currently under review is the payment of staff expenses.

For each of the following examples of expenses controls, match them to the most appropriate control activity from the list of pull down list options below:

Expenses claims are allocated to the relevant cost centre by entering the correct code for each claim onto the purchase ledger. [▼]

All expenses claim forms are printed on controlled stationery and stored in a locked cabinet which is only accessible via one of the cashiers. [▼]

The amount paid for each month's expenses run is shown as a separate line in the company's management accounts. [▼]

Employees are required to submit all expenses claims to their line manager before they can be paid. [▼]

Pull down list:

Authorisation
Information processing
Performance review
Physical controls
Segregation of duties

---

50 T is a government monitoring service and needs to operate and communicate in a secure online environment. Consequently, T has invested heavily in information technology controls.

Match the following terms extracted from their full description to the correct form of information technology control used by T from the list of pull down list options below:

'... you need access to a secret key or password to read it ...' [▼]

'... prevents unwelcome access to parts of the system ...' [▼]

'... adding an extra field to a message previously agreed by both parties ...'

[▼]

Pull down list:

Authentication
Encryption
Firewall

---

51 **Which ONE of the following items should NOT be in a SOC 2 report?**

- ○ A description of the controls in a service organisation
- ○ Assertions made by service organisation management about the controls in place
- ○ A list of the detailed tests carried out by the CPA
- ○ A statement that the report is limited to certain individuals

---

52 V is a new starter at a call centre and is required to access sensitive customer and product information but only for his own department as data protection is strictly regulated. As staff use a 'hot-desk' system (designed to allow flexible working conditions), passwords are required to ensure no employee can access information not assigned to them.

V was born in 1990, has a dog called 'Spike' and is often referred to as 'Vic' by his friends and family. His favourite food is cake and he is an avid follower of the Bloomsbury Bulldogs.

Which ONE of the following would be considered best practice for V to select an appropriate password?

- ○ Choosing 'vic1990' on his first day and writing it on the underside of his coffee mug.
- ○ Choosing 'BullDog2316' and setting an alert on his phone to change it in seven days' time.
- ○ Using the system-generated password on his first log-in to the system then sharing it with a colleague.
- ○ Using the system-generated password on his first log-in to the system, changing it to 'spike' and then setting an alert on his phone to change it in seven days' time.
- ○ Choosing 'viccake' and setting an alert on his phone to change it in seven days' time.

---

53 **Match the following features of a purchases system to the corresponding stages of that system using the list of pull down list options below:**

Controls exist to ensure that goods received notes (GRNs) are matched to orders before any action is taken. [▼]

Credit notes are reconciled to purchase ledger. [▼]

Requisitions are authorised by an approved signatory. [▼]

Pull down list:

Order
Receipt
Invoices and payment
Accounting

QUESTIONS

54 In 1973, Donald Cressey published a methodology for understanding the three factors that cause an individual to commit a fraud in the workplace:

- A pressure that motivates them to commit the fraud in the first place (pressure or motive)
- An opportunity to commit the fraud without detection (opportunity)
- The ability to rationalise the fraud so the perpetrator does not feel that a crime is being committed (rationalisation or dishonesty)

Cressey felt that understanding these factors better would allow organisations to protect themselves from the threat of fraud.

Match the following fraud prevention techniques with the most appropriate factor that each is attempting to address from the pull down list options below:

Seeking employment references for all new starters [▼]

Regular testing of the organisation's system of internal controls [▼]

Negotiation of pay and conditions with all employees [▼]

Pull down list:

Pressure or motive
Opportunity
Rationalisation or dishonesty

---

55 **Which of the following would be classed as inherent limitations of a system of internal controls?**

Select ALL that apply.

☐ Human error

☐ Segregation of duties

☐ Authorisation

☐ Management override

☐ Collusion

☐ Sampling risk

---

56 **Which of the following items would NOT be found within a contingency (or disaster recovery) plan used by an organisation in the event of a disaster?**

Select ALL that apply.

☐ Definition of responsibilities

☐ Budget

☐ Back-up arrangements

☐ Communication with staff

☐ Testing

☐ Risk assessment

---

57 You are the Senior Independent Director (SID) of Company W, a listed manufacturer of complex engineering parts, which has its own internal audit department. The head of internal audit reports to you as chair of the audit committee.

Which of the following criteria would you NOT take into account when assessing the performance of the internal auditors employed by Company W?

Select ALL that apply.

- ☐ The internal audit department's reporting lines
- ☐ The scope of the internal auditor's work
- ☐ The internal auditor's technical competence
- ☐ Cost savings identified by the internal auditor

---

58 **Which ONE of the following activities is least likely to be undertaken by internal auditors?**

- ○ Operational audits
- ○ Compliance audits
- ○ Computer system audits
- ○ Statutory audits

---

59 Company XX wishes to outsource its internal audit function.

Which of the following statements are true in this respect?

Select ALL that apply.

- ☐ Outsourcing the internal audit function means that the internal audit function will operate more efficiently and cost-effectively.
- ☐ Outsourcing the internal audit function may be more expensive than maintaining an in-house function.
- ☐ Outsourcing the internal audit function may result in the loss of control over the function.
- ☐ Outsourcing the internal audit function may involve making existing internal audit staff redundant.
- ☐ Outsourcing the internal audit function means that the directors of the company no longer have responsibility for the function.

---

60 **Which ONE of the following best describes the term 'social and environmental audit'?**

- ○ A process to establish whether or not an organisation secures economy, efficiency and effectiveness in its operations.
- ○ A process to establish whether or not an organisation complies with best practice and can be described as a good corporate citizen.
- ○ A process to establish whether or not an organisation delivers best value in its operations.
- ○ A process to establish whether or not an organisation achieves objectives in line with predetermined standards.

Practice mock answers

1 Answers

1 The correct answers are:

An event or events from which either good or bad outcomes could occur

Speculative risk ▼

A risk whose only possible outcome can be harmful. | Pure risk ▼ |

A risk that affects people in general which cannot be controlled by individuals

Fundamental risk ▼

An event or events from which either good or bad outcomes could occur, eg investment in infrastructure, may bring prosperity but may also lead to expensive assets laying idle = Speculative risk.

A risk whose only possible outcome can be harmful, eg the risks to passengers and crew from a plane crash, are pure risks = Pure risk.

A risk that affects people in general which cannot be controlled by individuals, eg climate change = Fundamental risk.

2 The correct answers are:

- Digital piracy
- Downloads to TVs, PCs and other digital devices

Strategic risk is the potential volatility of profits caused by the nature and type of the business strategies.

Digital piracy could lead to fewer people paying for films and revenues being adversely affected and as such this is a strategic risk.

Downloads to TVs, PCs and other digital devices (using services such as Amazon, Netflix and others) could stop people going to the cinema and buying a disc as they could stream a movie instead and X would not necessarily get the revenue and as such is a strategic risk.

A fall in the population's disposable income is unlikely to be long term or universal across many countries. The relative price of a cinema ticket is unlikely to make it seem a luxury item. The short-term nature and limited impact mean this is not a strategic risk.

Alternative technologies such as 3D or IMAX may vary the mix of revenue earned by X but is unlikely to affect the success of the film (many films that are released in 3D, for example, are also shown in 2D).

Demographic change within a country is again unlikely to affect X strategically as it appears to have diversified its products.

3 The correct answers are:

- Legal risk
- Reputation risk
- Litigation risk

Legal risk - not showing the safety demonstration may be a breach of legislation in a jurisdiction that Y flies through.

Reputation risk - not showing the safety demonstration may reduce customer confidence in Y's safety record which could affect future demand for its services.

Litigation risk - in the event of a crash, passengers may sue Y for not showing the safety demonstration, especially if harm has occurred as a result of such negligence.

Human hazard risk - this is the risk of a possible source of danger caused by human activity (such as terrorism or aircraft failure) and is unlikely to be managed by the in-house safety demonstration.

Employee risk - this could be either the risk to employees or the risk from employees as part of Y's normal activities. It is unlikely that the safety demonstration would affect risks to or from employees as passengers are still likely to require assistance outside of Y's normal activities in the event of a crash.

4 The correct answer is: Keep rates at 0.5%

Lobbying for change will lead to an expected value (EV) of interest payable based on the following calculations:

(0.25% × $70m) × 50% = $87,500

(0.75% × $150m) × 50% = $562,500

Total EV of interest payable = $650,000

Existing interest payable = 0.5% × $100m = $500,000

The bank would therefore opt to keep interest rates as they are and reduce the likely amount of interest payable to investors at the lower of these two values.

5 The correct answer is: Risk capacity

Risk capacity relates to the tangible and intangible assets that an asset has at its disposal to allow it to take risks and absorb losses.

Risk appetite is the amount of risk a business is willing to accept - this differs from risk capacity because it identifies the **desired** levels of risk, while risk capacity is more of a tolerable threshold that could be accommodated if necessary.

Risk attitude is a sub-set of risk appetite and refers to the level of risk considered desirable by an organisation and (frequently illustrated by deciding whether the business is risk seeking or risk averse).

Risk approach refers to the adoption of the enterprise risk management (ERM) model for assessment of risks.

6 The correct answers are:

- Aligned with all other activities
- Embedded within the organisation
- Limitations in available information actively considered
- Continual improvement through learning and experience

A commitment to risk management is listed as part of the risk management framework within ISO 31000, while recording and reporting is listed as part of the risk management process within ISO 31000.

7 The correct answer is: Transfer

It is most likely that B has transferred risk in this scenario, as it does not need to worry about sourcing components because it has transferred this risk to suppliers. If there was no contract in place, B could be described as only having reduced this risk by sourcing the components from a supplier that would reduce the risk of stock-out and may reduce the risk of cost (but not eliminate it).

8 The correct answer is: Pay the fine immediately but remove all workers until it is deemed safe

Being objective is not straightforward here and is likely to require careful thought - however, remembering that the company is not risk averse may help to clarify this for you. Vacating the mine and losing all assets is effectively abandoning the investment in P which does not embrace any risk at all (plus it will lead to significant losses that shareholders may be concerned about) so this option is unlikely.

Doing nothing might keep costs down in the short term, maintaining shareholder's interests due to the mine being so profitable, but is unlikely to placate the government in P, leading to calls that C is breaking the law and endangering the lives of workers in the mine, so as a longer term option, it appears unlikely too.

Paying the fine therefore seems appropriate, as it will allow C to continue trading both profitably and legally, avoiding losing its assets, but incurring some costs and reducing shareholder wealth. However, the options are differentiated by the importance of maintaining human life, which is C's highest policy priority, so workers should be moved out temporarily until guarantees (if any) are received that the mine can continue to operate.

9 The correct answers are:

- Entity level
- Division

Entity level and division are organisational levels that are referred to (the others are operation unit and function).

10 The correct answers are:

1 D is a campsite that posts notices for guests around its swimming pool that no lifeguards are on duty. [Transfer ▼]

2 E is an estate agency that has closed 10% of its branches due to a fiercely competitive sales environment. [Avoid ▼]

3 F is a doctor's surgery that sends its entire medical staff on regular and frequent training courses to improve their medical treatment skills. [Reduce ▼]

4 G is a nation that operates a space exploration programme and launches manned rockets four times a year to carry out experiments in zero gravity. [Accept ▼]

5 H is a supermarket that has recently suffered damage to its reputation due to errors in product labelling. As a result of this scandal, H has now changed suppliers for all affected products. [Reduce ▼]

D is a campsite that posts notices for guests around its swimming pool that no lifeguards are on duty (Transfer – risk is passed to guests, so the campsite is not liable in the event of an accident).

E is an estate agency that has closed 10% of its branches due to a fiercely competitive sales environment (Avoid – removing the business from an environment where risk can no longer be tolerated).

F is a doctor's surgery that sends its entire medical staff on regular and frequent training courses to improve their medical treatment skills (Reduce – better skills should mean that risk is reduced).

G is a nation that operates a space exploration programme and launches manned rockets four times a year to carry out experiments in zero gravity (Accept – no amount of control can reduce the risks associated with space exploration!).

H is a supermarket that has recently suffered damage to its reputation due to errors in product labelling. As a result of this scandal, H has now changed suppliers for all affected products (Reduce – you may think this is transferring risk but there is no mention of H being less liable as a result of this arrangement).

11 The correct answers are:

1 'I don't care about the costs, we need to increase throughput as much as possible to meet demand!' [Risk seeker ▼]

2 'I'm not happy with this course of action as the outcome does not match the effort required to achieve it.' [Risk averse ▼]

3 'My advice is to accept this course of action as that's what we did last year.' [Impossible to tell ▼]

4 'Considering the returns from this new product, I think we should explore the costs associated with it further.' [Risk averse ▼]

'I don't care about the costs, we need to increase throughput as much as possible to meet demand!' (Risk seeker, as the returns are the only focus here.)

'I'm not happy with this course of action as it looks like the outcome does not match the effort required to achieve it.' (Risk averse, as the risks are considered to be too high regardless of the fact that returns may rise.)

'My advice is to accept this course of action as that's what we did last year.' (Impossible to tell – we cannot tell what the advice was last year.)

'Considering the returns from this new product, I think we should explore the costs associated with it further.' (Risk averse – this sounds quite upbeat and risk seeking, but is actually only saying that we should assess risks in the context of returns, which is more in line with aversion.)

12 The correct answer is: Residual risk

By definition this is what residual risk means.

Gross risk is the amount of risk faced by an organisation before it deploys any risk management responses.

Balloon risk and post-response risks may be terms used in organisations, but they are not recognised within the CIMA official terminology.

13 The correct answers are:

- Profit-related pay
- Shares
- Executive share option plans

These methods link remuneration with company performance and hence encourage directors to maximise company value, in line with shareholder objectives. High basic salary and executive pension scheme contributions don't connect reward and performance.

14 The correct answer is: Being responsible for developing new investment initiatives.

This would normally be the responsibility of the chief executive officer (CEO).

15 The correct answer is: The nomination committee should consist entirely of executive directors.

Corporate governance practice varies, but the UK Corporate Governance Code recommends that the majority of a nomination committee should comprise independent non-executive directors.

16 The correct answer is: Integrity

The definition is taken from the CIMA Code of Ethics (but is also relevant to corporate governance best practice).

17 The correct answer is: Self-review

This is a case of self-review threat, meaning that MM is unlikely to be suitably sceptical about his workings and may not consider the calculations from a broad enough perspective to make the review effective.

18 The correct answer is: The code is perceived by staff as inflexible.

This may make the code unpopular, but it does not make it difficult to enforce.

The other options suggest that it will be difficult to enforce the code as it is.

19 The correct answer is: Governance and culture

Governance and culture requires the board to take formal ownership of risk oversight - although a risk appetite has been set, it is not stated that this has board approval. The remaining elements of COSO have been adopted.

20 The correct answers are:

- Establishing a common risk management language
- Providing leadership, vision and direction for enterprise risk management

Providing leadership, vision and direction of enterprise risk management and establishing a common risk management language are both recognised elements of a risk manager's role.

Risk appetite may be quantified by a risk manager, but it is set by the board in consultation with investors.

Similarly, the risk manager may advise the board about enterprise risk management but will not decide its approach.

21 The correct answers are:

- The materials used in manufacture
- The employment conditions in supplier workplaces
- The packaging used

Consumers increasingly expect products to be produced and packaged using materials, components and packaging that have been sourced and/or produced ethically. Sustainability and recyclability are key concerns.

Price may have social impacts but is more likely to be outside of the manufacturer's control while the relative merits of competitor products are issues of a purely commercial nature.

22 The correct answers are:

- Remuneration arrangements
- The provision of non-audit services
- Assessment of objectivity and independence
- Communicating errors in the draft financial statements

Assessment of the control environment is an activity performed by the external auditor as part of the statutory audit, while determining the organisation's risk appetite is carried out by the board of directors.

23 The correct answer is: Products are more easily available at a cheaper price than using other online retailers.

Products can be ordered using the website 24/7 - this doesn't mention price, plus A is not the only online retailer, so this statement doesn't differentiate A from other retailers either.

Products are cheapest on A's website - this statement doesn't mention A's superior availability or customer service which are both part of its brand.

Buying products from A means you agree with their values - this statement is more likely to describe the impact on their reputation, not their brand.

24 The correct answer is: Adverse reputation risk

Global social media means these stories can easily be accessed by stakeholders, leading to heightened reputation risk.

Increased litigation risk in the developing countries is unlikely as their health and safety standards are not likely to be as strict as they are in C's country.

Adverse impact on the company's supply chain is unlikely, as labour is likely to be easily available in the developing countries where C is experiencing problems.

Overspending on its advertising budgets is also unlikely: although C may wish to promote the positive side of its business, the company is unlikely to want to publicise these events, so will not draw attention to them in its advertising.

25 The correct answers are:

- Dodd-Frank
- Basel III

Dodd-Frank is the US version, while Basel III is the globally recognised authority on banking supervision. Sarbanes-Oxley relates to corporate governance in the USA, while ISO 31000 is the international standard for risk management.

26 The correct answers are:

- Shortage of fossil fuels
- Changes in government legislation
- Rise of electric and hybrid engines

The shortage of fossil fuels means that F needs to develop alternative ways of powering their vehicles once reserves are exhausted. Changes in government legislation mean that emissions and other targets could limit existing operations if F is unable to comply. The rise of electric and hybrid engines represents competition which is growing, so F either needs to join in or innovate.

While raw material prices, over-capacity in production and international trade tariffs are also legitimate concerns for F, they are not technology-related (and hence are not considered to disrupt F as much as the correct options).

27 The correct answer is: The investment may not deliver the required returns

The investment may not deliver the required returns because in a declining market, this cash-cow has reached maturity and has become a dog, as the market is in decline due to increasing demand for digital downloads that do not require physical storage.

Customer demand will not put pressure on A's production capacity as demand is falling.

The extra marketing spend will not have a detrimental impact on profits as it has the same product in a declining market, so there is no point in increasing A's marketing activity.

Additional market research testing will not affect profits because the same product will not require the need to test the market.

28 The correct answer is: Increasing demand for streaming

More consumers are accessing content digitally than ever before, so the impact of streaming on traditional techniques for delivering content (such as H) is significant.

Competition from online retailers of CDs, DVDs and Blu-rays is a valid reason for H's strategy being disrupted, but it is not new and ignores the increase in streaming.

There is no evidence from the scenario that an app or website would help H.

There is also no evidence that illegal copies of CDs, DVDs and Blu-rays are a disruption, as they affect all retailers selling these products, not just H, and this ignores the decline in these physical media and the threat posed by digital downloads, which is where the syllabus is focused.

29 The correct answers are:

- Value at risk
- Net present value

Value at risk models the maximum expected losses in line with normal probability levels, while net present value models all cash flows adjusted for risk.

Sensitivity analysis only looks at individual elements rather than the whole, so would not be appropriate for a new product launch, while payback only estimates the time for investment to be repaid and is not risk adjusted (although knowledge of the timescales involved could be considered helpful as part of stress testing).

30 The correct answer is: Change in government

A change in government policy could lead to fewer contracts being awarded.

Economic uncertainty is less likely to affect Company C as people still need hospitals and bridges. Consumer tastes may change but people still need hospitals and bridges. An increase in digital technology may affect some public services (for example, allowing for more online or virtual diagnosis) but overall people still need the services that hospitals and bridges provide.

31 The correct answers are:

- Customer date of birth
- Customer email address
- Employee pay details
- Employee addresses

Company addresses are likely to be available on the company's website, while the company's registration details are likely to be available from the local registrar of companies.

32 The correct answer is: Company products - these can usually be found on a company's website

The remaining options are all more likely to lead to some form of cybersecurity risk due to the information being considered sensitive in some way.

33 The correct answer is: Confidentiality

Confidentiality means ensuring that legitimately available data is protected from unauthorised access (ie objectives for closing it off).

Availability means accessible, but only to those with the right to have it, for legitimate purposes only (ie objectives for opening it up).

Integrity of data means accurate, intelligible, reliable, not lost, not corrupted.

Integrity of processing means not used for illegal or immoral purposes, not used in a way that the data subject did not intend.

34 The correct answer is: Identifying gaps in cybersecurity so they can be addressed before they create a threat

Unethical hackers exploit gaps in cybersecurity for their own purposes.

Grey hat hackers offer to fix a cybersecurity threat for a fee but may post the weakness online if the offer is not taken up.

Social engineering is exploiting someone's trust to gain illegal access to personal data.

35 The correct answers are:

- Hacking
- Ransomware
- Spyware

Infected memory sticks, unauthorised websites accessed by staff, illegally obtained software and employees with a grudge against the organisation all originate from inside the organisation.

36 The correct answer is: Hunt team

Hunt teams seek out as yet unidentified cybersecurity breaches.

Insider threat teams attempt to intercept internal threats.

Threat intelligence teams attempt to intercept external threats.

Incident response teams deal with the immediate aftermath of any breach and are generally known as either computer incident response teams (CIRTs) or computer security incident response teams (CSIRTs).

37 The correct answer is: Breaking binary code apart for the purposes of responding to a malware threat

Converting binary code into assembler code for the purposes of responding to a malware threat is disassembly.

Converting binary code into source code for the purposes of responding to a malware threat is decompilation.

Breaking binary code into separate streams to allow more than one person to analyse it may sound plausible but is not the definition of reverse engineering.

38 The correct answer is: Phishing

Hacking is where servers have been illegally accessed and confidential personal data from customers obtained.

Ransomware is where access to sensitive data is withheld unless a payment is made.

Distributed denial of service attack is where online operations have been suspended due to excessive amounts of false enquiries which the system cannot cope with.

39 The correct answer is: Service level agreement (SLA)

Intranets tend to be used by internal staff not external users. Workplace learning is unlikely to be available for external users. Face-to-face meetings are unlikely to be run by Company F for external users.

40 The correct answers are:

- Due diligence
- Contracts

Employing an external law firm to select each one would not help, as it is unlikely they would possess the right expertise to help with this. Having a sponsor at board level is too high up the organisation for such a decision to be taken, while obtaining references from other customers would not be definitive enough.

41 The correct answer is: Information committee

An information committee might be useful but is not specifically mentioned in ISO 27001.

42 The correct answer is: The analysis will determine whether a breach has occurred and confirm the cause, culprits and consequences.

Determining the cause, culprits and consequences of the breach is incorrect because it has not been confirmed that there is a breach yet: it is only suspected so far.

Determining whether a breach has occurred and confirming the consequences does not go far enough: the analysis should also confirm the cause and culprits.

Confirming the extent of the breach by analysing the malware to identify its source assumes the breach has occurred and doesn't consider cause or consequence.

43 The correct answers are:

- Market share
- Brand values
- Competitor profitability
- Cash flow
- New entrants in the market

These are all examined using strategic management accounting. You may have been tempted to discount the last option ('new entrants in the market') as it is an element of Porter's Five Forces model, but anything to do with the competitive environment is relevant to this holistic approach.

44 The correct answers are:

Overtime paid to machine operatives [Process time ▼]

Complaints from customers [Quality ▼]

Complaints from retailers [Delivery ▼]

Machine downtime [Process time ▼]

Overtime is most likely to be an indicator of the production process taking too long.

Complaints will vary - those from customers are most likely to be about quality, while those from retailers will mostly relate to successful delivery of products. Retailers are not the end user of the products and are therefore less likely to be directly affected by quality and more likely to be directly affected by delivery delays.

Machine downtime is most likely to indicate the risk of production processes being slowed down by faulty machinery, hence process time is most likely here.

45 The correct answers are:

Buying in bulk to address adverse price variances

[Adverse inventory holding costs ▼]

Additional production to improve labour efficiency

[Adverse inventory amounts ▼]

Product re-working to reduce the percentage of products failing final quality checks

[Adverse productivity levels ▼]

Buying in bulk does reduce unit costs for raw materials but holding such levels of inventory can be expensive and may outweigh the benefits of the purchases savings made.

Increasing levels of production may make better use of labour that would otherwise be idle but can lead to excess levels of production which will increase the level of stock until they can be sold or despatched.

Re-working products to meet quality standards may reduce non-conformance costs but may adversely affect the levels of productivity enjoyed by the business to a disproportionate effect.

46 The correct answers are:

'An efficient system that helps avoid information overload by highlighting key information only, usually by setting parameters from which management action is likely to be required, such as overspending which exceeds budget by 5%.' [Exception reporting ▼]

'This is an enhancement to our existing reporting structure that allows users to start with a macro view of our entire business and then focus on specific key areas by applying more of a micro-approach to a variety of activities.' [Drill down report ▼]

'The starting point for all users, showing all activity and performance in a summarised and sometimes graphical manner, supported by financial and non-financial information sourced from a variety of parts of the company.' [Executive dashboard ▼]

The key to selecting 'exception reporting' is the use of terms such as 'parameters' and 'exceed'.

A drill down report allows users to focus on a specific area by starting at a more global level and then 'drilling down' into the detail.

Executive dashboards - the key to this is probably the word 'graphical'.

If you selected 'Full cost accounting report' you suggested the use of a report that breaks down costs into environmental and other elements (such as the cost of packaging, clean-up costs, fines for hazardous emissions etc).

If you selected 'Balanced scorecard', this is a technique that uses four key measures for optimal business performance: financial; innovation, customer focus; and quality of processes.

47 The correct answers are:

Performance-related pay for an executive director of a retailer where performance is based on market share and sales targets. [Effective ▼]

A discretionary bonus paid to air traffic controllers for ensuring all flights take off from the airport where they are based on schedule. [Ineffective ▼]

A manufacturer of mobile telecommunication processors employs quality control inspectors who run a specialised test on a sample of processors from each production run. Inspectors are paid a basic salary plus a variable amount for each faulty item identified.

[Ineffective ▼]

Performance-related pay for an executive director of a retailer where performance is based on market share and sales targets is usually a key part of sound governance, aligning individual rewards with corporate objectives to encourage goal congruent behaviour.

A discretionary bonus paid to air traffic controllers for ensuring all flights take off from the airport where they are based on schedule may seem like a good idea, but ignores the fact that circumstances outside the employee's control – such as weather, engine failure and security issues – may mean that this target can never be hit and so may either de-motivate or even encourage excessive risk-taking just to hit the target.

A manufacturer of mobile telecommunication processors employs quality control inspectors who run a specialised test on a sample of processors from each production run. Inspectors are paid a basic salary plus a variable amount for each faulty item identified. Again, this sounds like it is motivating employees to identify poor quality products, but the company is actually basing rewards on criteria that are easy for the employee to manipulate and as such this specialised test may be fixed by the quality control staff to ensure a higher number of processors fail in order to increase their rewards.

48 The correct answer is: A procedures manual for paying wages and salaries

This question is specifically looking at an organisation's 'control environment'. The key to this question is understanding the term 'environment' - this is the overall tone, the culture, the values and the expected behaviours of the company, not the specific physical controls such as reconciliations, authorisation, ticking boxes etc.

The behaviours and beliefs of the directors will affect the overall environment, setting the 'tone from the top'.

The structure of the entity and how staff are supervised either loosely or closely will affect the overall control environment.

The presence and effectiveness of internal audit will again affect the company-wide attitude to controls.

A code of conduct does affect the staff behaviour, attitudes and therefore the environment/culture.

A procedures manual is a specific control procedure showing detailed controls in place for the payroll system. This is the only option within this question which does not affect the control environment. All of the others affect attitudes and culture. A control procedure shows detail in a specific area, not the global control environment.

49 The correct answers are:

Expenses claims are allocated to the relevant cost centre by entering the correct code for each claim onto the purchase ledger. Information processing ▼

All expenses claim forms are printed on controlled stationery and stored in a locked cabinet which is only accessible via one of the cashiers. Physical controls ▼

The amount paid for each month's expenses run is shown as a separate line in the company's management accounts. Performance review ▼

Employees are required to submit all expenses claims to their line manager before they can be paid. Authorisation ▼

Expenses claims are allocated to the relevant cost centre by entering the correct code for each claim onto the purchase ledger. This is a straightforward information processing control for an application where inputs are processed.

All expenses claim forms are printed on controlled stationery and stored in a locked cabinet which is only accessible via one of the cashiers. While a separate member of staff is required for this, it is not an example of segregation of duties because the key control relates to the need to gain access to a unique sequentially numbered claim form, not the need for someone else to access it.

The amount paid for each month's expenses run is shown as a separate line in the company's management accounts. This is a straightforward example of performance review, where the budget holder will compare actual spend versus budget and investigate any unusual variances.

Employees are required to submit all expenses claims to their line manager before they can be paid. Again, this is likely to be a straightforward case of authorisation by a senior member of staff.

50 The correct answers are:

'... you need access to a secret key or password to read it ...' Encryption ▼

'... prevents unwelcome access to parts of the system ...' Firewall ▼

'... adding an extra field to a message previously agreed by both parties ...'
Authentication ▼

'*... you need access to a secret key or password to read it ...*' Encryption translates a message into secret code that can only be read with a secret key or password to decrypt it. It is not authentication as it relates to reading, not access.

'*... prevents unwelcome access to parts of the system ...*' A firewall is a system designed to prevent unauthorised access to or from a private network. Firewalls can be implemented in both hardware and software, or a combination of both.

'*... adding an extra field to a message previously agreed by both parties ...*' Authentication ensures that messages have come from authorised senders by using an extra field agreed between two parties: without it, the message will be disregarded. It is not encryption as there is no suggestion that the message cannot be read, unlike the first option.

51 The correct answer is: A description of the controls in a service organisation

SOC 2 does not require a description of the controls in a service organization - the remaining options all relate to a SOC 2 report.

52 The correct answer is: Choosing 'BullDog2316' and setting an alert on his phone to change it in seven days' time.

'vic1990' is too obvious a password (nickname and year of birth) plus writing it down is poor control.

Using the system-generated password is good practice but it should not be shared with anyone.

Similarly, changing it to 'spike' is likely to be easy to guess from limited knowledge of V.

'viccake' is slightly stronger as it uses two discrete pieces of information about V and will be changed in seven days, but using 'BullDog2316' is stronger as it uses a mixture of lower and upper case text and is also alphanumeric.

53 The correct answers are:

Controls exist to ensure that goods received notes (GRNs) are matched to orders before any action is taken.	Invoices and payment ▼
Credit notes are reconciled to purchase ledger.	Accounting ▼
Requisitions are authorised by an approved signatory.	Order ▼

Controls exist to ensure that goods received notes (GRNs) are matched to orders before any action is taken. Invoices should only be paid once the order has been matched to evidence that the goods have actually been received.

Credit notes are reconciled to purchase ledger. Usually these relate to retrospective adjustments required once a payment has been made (eg if goods are found to be faulty and the supplier refunds the amount involved) which need to be included within that supplier's record on the purchase ledger.

Requisitions are authorised by an approved signatory. This should be an example of a control that exists to ensure that orders are not allowed to be processed without suitable authorisation by the company.

54 The correct answers are:

Seeking employment references for all new starters	Rationalisation or dishonesty ▼
Regular testing of the organisation's system of internal controls	Opportunity ▼
Negotiation of pay and conditions with all employees	Pressure or motive ▼

ANSWERS

Seeking employment references for all new starters. It is not possible to be 100% effective but seeking references for new employees should identify those who have a criminal record, or have been disciplined for similar offences in the past, and who therefore may be inherently more likely to re-offend.

Regular testing of the organisation's system of internal controls. This should reduce the opportunity for fraud to be committed by ensuring that systems are more likely to prevent as well as detect fraud.

Negotiation of pay and conditions with all employees. Again, this is unlikely to be 100% effective, but ensuring that staff are not unhappy or bearing a grudge against their employer makes it less likely that they will steal from them.

55 The correct answers are:

- Human error
- Management override
- Collusion

Human error, management override (being asked to do something against the rules by management) and collusion (working with another member of staff to circumvent controls such as segregation of duties) are all inherent limitations of systems of internal controls. Other inherent limitations would also include unforeseen circumstances and the cost of a system outweighing the benefits derived from that system.

Segregation of duties and authorisation are both specific forms of internal control so cannot be limitations.

Sampling risk is the likelihood that an auditor will derive a different conclusion from a sample than that of the population - while it is an inherent risk of the sampling work undertaken by internal auditors, for example, it is not an inherent limitation of that system.

56 The correct answers are:

- Budget
- Testing

There are two items listed above that may be considered when implementing a contingency plan - budget and testing - but neither of these is part of the content of the actual plan itself:

- Budget would be allocated before the plan was compiled.
- Testing would be undertaken periodically to ensure the plan was effective, but would not form part of the plan used in the event of a disaster.

A typical contingency plan will consist of the following stages:

- Definition of responsibilities (taking control in a crisis and delegating tasks to others)
- Priorities (identifying which parts of the crisis should be addressed first)
- Back up arrangements (methods used to restore data and processing as soon as possible)
- Communication with staff (to ensure effective implementation of the contingency plan and 'joined up' responses)
- Public relations (to manage information required by the public and/or media)
- Risk assessment (an ongoing assessment of the crisis to determine progress or escalation)

57 The correct answer is: Cost savings identified by the internal auditor

The internal audit department will be assessed on the strength of its independence, meaning that any reporting lines that go directly to senior management may lack objectivity.

Similarly, the scope of the work undertaken by the internal auditors and their technical competence in the area of complex engineering will also be important in assessing both the quality of their work and the role they play in supporting the audit committee.

Cost savings are important to any organisation, but simply identifying them does not necessarily mean that the internal audit department has been effective - more cost savings may be achievable, but the internal auditors may have missed them, plus cost savings alone do not necessarily lead to increased profits for the company.

58 The correct answer is: Statutory audits

While it is possible that the range of activities encompassed by the term 'statutory audits' may be very broad, it is most likely to include a company's external audit or some other form of regulated inspection, which by definition is likely to require the services of an independent external auditor.

The other three options are all far more likely to be completed by an internal auditor:

- Operational audits (ensuring risk and control within normal operations are managed by means of both having sound policies and ensuring they work effectively)
- Compliance audits (ensuring that internal procedures are operating in line with predetermined requirements)
- Computer system audits (ensuring that computer systems are operating as intended)

Remember to read the question, which in this case asked for the ONE activity that internal audit would be LEAST LIKELY to undertake.

59 The correct answers are:

- Outsourcing the internal audit function may be more expensive than maintaining an in-house function.
- Outsourcing the internal audit function may result in the loss of control over the function.
- Outsourcing the internal audit function may involve making existing internal audit staff redundant.

Outsourcing an internal audit function (like any other form of outsourcing) is not guaranteed to make any savings in the cost of that function, and may even be more expensive. It may also result in a loss of control with the audit function being provided by a third party rather than direct reports/employees. Outsourcing may lead to existing staff being made redundant, although this is not always the case.

The most important point to note, however, is that simply outsourcing a function does not automatically remove the responsibility for it. The directors of a company will retain overall responsibility for the control and risk frameworks but assurance on the risks and controls will be provided by an outsourced internal audit function. Overall responsibility cannot be delegated, but the work can.

60 The correct answer is: A process to establish whether or not an organisation complies with best practice and can be described as a good corporate citizen.

Social and environmental audits are a means of assessing whether an entity's activities and disclosures relating to corporate social responsibility (CSR) are reasonable. The correct answer is that these types of audits describe a process to establish whether or not an organisation complies with best practice and can be described as a good corporate citizen.

A process to establish whether or not an organisation secures economy, efficiency and effectiveness in its operations is a value for money audit.

A process to establish whether or not an organisation delivers best value in its operations is an application of value for money auditing often seen in the public sector.

A process to establish whether or not an organisation achieves objectives in line with predetermined standards is most likely to be a quality audit.